WHY NO GOSPELS IN TALMUDIC JUDAISM?

Number 135
Why No Gospels in Talmudic Judaism?

by
Jacob Neusner

Why No Gospels in Talmudic Judaism?

by
Jacob Neusner

Scholars Press
Atlanta, Georgia

Why No Gospels in Talmudic Judaism?

©1988
Brown University

Library of Congress Cataloging in Publication Data

Neusner, Jacob, 1932-
      Why no gospels in Talmudic Judaism? / Jacob Neusner.
        p. cm. -- (Brown Judaic studies ; no. 135)
      ISBN 1-555-40198-8. ISBN 1-555-40199-6 (pbk.)
      1. Talmud -- Philosophy. 2. Tradition (Judaism) I. Title
      II. Series.
      BM501.N485 1988   *L9776*
      296.1'2066--dc19

Printed in the United States of America
on acid-free paper

In memory of

JOHN ALLEN FRERICHS

(1951-1987)

Everyone who knew him as he grew up
in the family of his parents and their
university community and colleagues
remembers with admiration his remarkable
capacity to overcome the troubles of the age
and to make a life for himself, and on his own,
against it all, despite it all. Remembering him
is to celebrate courage and hope,
the overcoming of adversity,
the renewal and the affirmation of life.

That is his legacy and the inheritance he left us all.

Mourning, with his bereaved parents, brother, sister,
and family, the years he did not live, all of those who love
them and cherished his friendship and admired his life
are thankful, at the very least, for the years that he did live.
And we look forward to solace for his kith and kin,
who, remembering, mourn but also celebrate,
grieve and also give thanks.

That is what it means to be a Frerichs,
and to be one of the privileged circle of those instructed and informed by their love.

This book goes to press within thirty days of his death,
only one among the many monuments to his well-lived life.

TABLE OF CONTENTS

PREFACE

These five free-standing essays, all published here for the first time, address colleagues in the history of religion with special interest in the comparative study of Christianity and Judaism in their formative centuries. I ask a simple question: why does Christianity produce gospels and lives of saints and Judaism does not? My focus is on the negatives[1]. What I claim to explain is the absence, in the Judaism of the dual Torah, of gospels. I show that the raw materials for the formation of gospels, specifically, stories of miracles done by holy men, as well as the finished materials, well-composed stories about sages, came in ample supply within the Judaism of the dual Torah. But stories of holy men's miracles were not woven into lives of holy men, nor was a holy man represented as the model for the imitation of all others in the way in which, in the Gospels, Jesus Christ was represented by the Evangelists, and that simple difference between the Judaism of the dual Torah and the Christianity of the Gospels is what I wish to explain. The program of the book is simple.

After a brief account, in Chapter One, of the character of the Judaism of the dual Torah, oral and written, which, by reference to its principal document, the Talmud of Babylonia or Bavli, I here call "talmudic Judaism," I draw together two intersecting themes, miracle and magic, on the one side, sustained biographies of holy men bearing the message of the faith, such as we call gospels, on the other. The second essay shows that the Judaism that took shape in the first six centuries of the Common Era (=A.D.) represented some of its holy men as miracle workers just as much as diverse Christianities represented Jesus and saints as holy persons. Accordingly, the raw materials for the creation of the same sort of lives of saints as Christianity produced were available to Judaic writers. Not only so, but in the second and third papers I show that the themes of wonder-working, within the larger and encompassing topic of the lives of saints or holy persons, animated story-telling, as evidenced in the literary heritage of the Judaism under study. Accordingly, I demonstrate that the prerequisites of the formation of gospels — miracle-stories, the telling of biographical stories, not merely the preservation of aphorisms and other sayings — flourished in the Judaism of the dual Torah as much as in the Christianities represented by our extant writings.

And that sets forth the question of the comparison of religions, Christianity and Judaism in their formative ages, with which I deal. I spell out my answer in Chapter Four. Why is it that Christianity produced gospels, Judaism did not? To answer that question I appeal to the quite different tasks undertaken by holy persons, with the Judaic sages assigned the work of public policy, the Christian saints differentiated

[1]But of course the traits are not negative or positive and the comparison is not invidious. I do not think that a religion that produces gospels is better or truer than one that does not, nor that a religion that produces philosophy, including science, is more worthwhile than one that does not. I ask only what we understand about two religions when we compare them at points that permit comparison, and how we understand each more adequately when we compare it to some other.

from other sorts of Christian authorities altogether. The sage also governed; the saint rarely governed. The model of the sage derived from Moses, our rabbi, who led Israel, God's holy people. The model of the saint accord with the example of Jesus, the crucified and risen Christ, one and unique, to be imitated in his holiness, not to be expected to sort out the affairs of the everday Christian world. The capacity of Christianity to differentiate what in the Judaism of the dual Torah formed an indivisible union, the life of the faith in the city of heaven from the life of the state in the city on earth, corresponds to the focus, within Christianity, on individuals in the model of Christ to be imitated. The insistence of the Judaism of the dual Torah that the sage bore public, and not only exemplary, responsibilities, accounts for the representation of the sage as never solitary and individual, but always exemplary and at the service of the community. In literary terms, Christian holy books had authors, Judaic ones, solely authorships, as I shall explain in Chapter Four.

As I shall show, the same kinds of stories were told about sages as about Jesus. Both the Judaic sage and Jesus as portrayed in Gospels worked wonders and did things that, under other circumstances, magicians were believed able to do. Accordingly, miracles and magic formed the themes The point of comparison is a simple one, and I mean to set forth the Judaic side of the equation. Christianity created many gospels about its principal figure, of which four became canonical. Later on, compiling and writing lives of saints were a common mode of religious statement. The Judaism of the dual Torah, which, among many candidates, emerged from late antiquity as the normative Judaism created no gospel. What I mean is simply that we have no book (or equivalent, for example, a sustained life story) about a single sage among the hundreds mentioned in the rabbinic literature. That fact stands for a still larger trait of the Judaic system of the dual Torah, that none of its formative documents bears the marks of original authorship. The simple failure to sign one's name to one's own writing represents only the surface. In matters of form, rhetorical traits, as well as logic, and in significant measure, even in the thematic program, no document of the canon of Judaism bears the marks of a singular and personal author. All stand for the consensus of authors I call an "authorship." That literary fact represents the larger social reality to which I made reference: the community of Israel, God's holy people, appealed to the whole, the commonality, making slight place for the holy man except as exemplary, never as unique, and for the holy woman not at all. By contrast, the community of Church, the body of Christ, referred to the unique figure of Jesus Christ, the one and only God in the flesh, who is to be not only worshipped and revered, but also imitated — in all his individuality. So the one system made no provision for what lay at the center of the structure of the other, which is the radically-defined individual. Accordingly, the thesis and the arguments follows a simple pattern. First I show what might have been. Then I begin the process of explaining what was, or, more to the point, what never came into being. Obviously, in these four simple essays I only lay out what I think are promising paths of inquiry. But the single idea that emerges through the sequence of arguments and analyses seems to me an interesting one, not unworthy of the reader's attention.

ii

PREFACE

In the final essay, Chapter Five, I develop in its own terms the alternative to the gospel or the life of the saint as a mode of making a religious statement. I point out that talmudic Judaism sets forth a large-scale and orderly system, general rules governing diverse cases, in the manner of philosophy. The Mishnah, which I describe as a systemic and systematic statement, serves in my mind as the alternative to a gospel. The gospel or the life of a saint deals with one person, the Mishnah with the entire community. The gospel or life of a saint emphasizes the exemplary character of the individual, the Mishnah, the governing status of rules affecting everyone. In contrasting a gospel with the Mishnah, I mean only to underline that in these two closely associated, scriptural religions, we nonetheless deal with two utterly distinct, not merely distinctive, religious systems: different people talking about different things to different people, with nothing much in common. So talmudic Judaism did not produce gospels because it was Judaism, not Christianity: and the two never met. But they do today, which is all the more reason to reckon with the essential and fundamental difference between the two. When we undertake to compare them, we realize that each scarcely sustains comparison with the other. And when we realize that simple, naked fact, the future starts.

It remains to thank my co-worker, Professors Ernest S. Frerichs and Wendell S. Dietrich, Brown University, Professor William Scott Green, University of Rochester, and Professor Paul Flesher, Wittenberg University, for their advice in planning this book, and Professor Robert Berchman, Michigan State University, for his counsel on philosophical matters. My colleague Professor Dietrich underlined for me the peculiarity, for Christian theological resonance, of spelling gospel with a small g, just as, in my Incarnation of God, he stressed the odd sound of spelling incarnation with a small i. In Christianity, rightly understood, there can be only the Gospel of Jesus Christ, and no other gospels, and the Incarnation of Jesus Christ, a unique event. In insisting on comparing religions, so reducing capital letters to small letters and treating "gospel" and "incarnation" as categories accessible to other religious traditions, I mean no disrespect to the faith of Christian believers, which I honor.

At this point in my *ouevre*, it may seem redundant to call attention, also, to all that I enjoy from the collegiality of the best colleagues who ever lived, in alphabetical order, Wendell S. Dietrich, Ernest S. Frerichs, and Calvin Goldscheider. Not be ordered in the scale of value, each bears his own distinctive traits and therefore, to me and to many others, brings each his own special gifts. I vastly value them all and cannot tire of expressing my thanks to them for endowing the everyday with those enjoyments of mind and also heart that less fortunate people look forward to knowing only in *yeshiva shel maalah*.

Jacob Neusner

	Program in Judaic Studies
July 28, 1987	Brown University
My fifty-fifth birthday	Providence, Rhode Island 02912-1826 U.S.A.

iii.

CHAPTER ONE
LITERATURE AND SOCIETY:
THE TALMUD IN ITS HISTORICAL AND THEOLOGICAL
CONTEXT

I. ORIGIN, NATURE, AND FUNCTION OF THE TALMUD

Since Talmudic Judaism defines the Judaism under discussion here, let us begin with an account of that Judaism, its literary evidence and its social setting. In this way colleagues who specialize in other literatures will have in hand the facts they require to follow the argument of this book. There are in fact two Talmuds, both of which serve as a commentary upon, and expansion of, the Mishnah[1]. The Mishnah is a philosophical law code, produced in the Land of Israel ("Palestine") in ca. A.D. 200. The first Talmud to the Mishnah was formed in the Land of Israel in ca. A.D. 400, and is called "the Talmud of the Land of Israel" or "the Jerusalem Talmud," and, in Hebrew, "the Yerushalmi." This Talmud covers thirty-nine of the Mishnah's sixty-two tractates. The second Talmud to that same Mishnah was created in Babylonia, which corresponds to present day Iraq, around Baghdad, in ca. A.D. 600, and is called "the Talmud of Babylonia," and, in Hebrew, "the Bavli." This one treats thirty-seven of the Mishnah's sixty-two tractates, and not the same tractates as the other. Both Talmuds to the one Mishnah consist of a series of citations of Mishnah-paragraphs and systematic, carefully drafted explanations of words and phrases of the Mishnah-passage, followed by secondary expansions of principles of the Mishnah-passage. Each Talmud may therefore be described as a commentary to the Mishnah, and both are organized in commentary-form. The Bavli, in addition, builds sizable compositions around systematic interpretation of passages of Scripture, which is read within the same basic approaches as apply to the Mishnah. Because the Bavli presents an ample restatement of the important principles of both Scripture and the Mishnah, it is the more compendious of the two Talmuds and also the more influential. Consequently, when people refer to "the Talmud," they mean "the Bavli." But we shall treat both, since each is a Talmud.

II. THE TALMUDS AND THE TORAH: THE THEOLOGICAL CONTEXT

Defined theologically, the Talmuds form part of the Torah, that is to say, God's revelation to Moses at Mount Sinai. We can understand the Bavli, its origin, character, and influence as the single most authoritative document of Judaism, only within that theological context. For the Bavli constitutes the authoritative statement of the Torah as the Torah would be read in Judaism from antiquity to modern times. To explain that fundamental conception of Judaism, from which all else follows, we ask how the Bavli is deemed part of the Torah. The answer lies in the meaning of the word "Torah." It bears the simple meaning of God's revelation. At Sinai,

---

[1]This chapter is a substantial revision of my entry, "Talmud," in *International Standard Bible Encyclopedia* (Wm. B. Eerdmans Publishing Co.).

Judaism maintains, God revealed the Torah in two media, writing and memory. The written Torah corresponds to the Hebrew Scriptures or the Old Testament. The memorized, or oral, Torah was orally formulated and orally transmitted for many centuries, from Moses to Joshua to prophets and sages and ultimately to the authorities who composed the Mishnah. That is the account of the origin and authority of the Mishnah given in tractate Avot, the founders' sayings, formed in ca. A.D. 250, about a generation after the completion of the Mishnah in ca. A.D. 200. That systematic statement commences, "Moses received Torah at Sinai and handed it on to Joshua, Joshua to the prophets, " and onward to the sages. Each name that is listed is given a saying, e.g., "If I not for myself, who will be for me? If I am only for myself, what am I? If not now, when?" assigned to Hillel, who flourished toward the turn of the first century A.D. Since the list of sages of Avot continues right on through important figures in the Mishnah itself, the position of the authorship of Avot is that sages of the Mishnah stand in a direct line to Sinai. And it further follows that the Mishnah constitutes a statement of the oral, or memorized, Torah of Sinai.

Commentaries and expansions of the Mishnah, as much as of Scripture, therefore fall into the classification of Torah — statements within the revelation of God to Moses at Mount Sinai. Since the Talmud, meaning the Bavli, comes at the end of the process of expansion and amplification of both the Mishnah and also Scripture — oral and written Torah, respectively — the Bavli forms the authoritative and final statement, for the formative period of Judaism, of the Torah.

III. THE BAVLI IN LITERARY CONTEXT

A brief account of the writings between the Mishnah and the Bavli will place into context that authoritative and conclusive statement of the whole. The writings of the sages between the Mishnah and the Bavli, ca. A.D. 200 and 600, fall into two distinct groups, one beginning with the Mishnah and ending about two centuries later, in 400, with the Tosefta and close associates of the Mishnah; the other beginning with the Yerushalmi in ca. A.D.400 and ending about two centuries later, with the Bavli. The Mishnah, as we know, drew in its wake tractate Abot, a statement of concluded a generation after the Mishnah on the standing of the authorities of the Mishnah. Attached to the Mishnah also is the Tosefta, ca.A.D. 300-400, a compilations of supplements of various kinds to the statements in the Mishnah. There were also three systematic exegeses of books of Scripture or the written Torah, tied to the Mishnah because, in passages, they may cite the Mishnah or the Tosefta verbatim and raise interesting questions about the relationship between the Mishnah or the Tosefta and Scripture. These works are the Sifra, to Leviticus, Sifré to Numbers, and another Sifré, to Deuteronomy. These books overall form one stage in the unfolding of the Judaism of the dual Torah, oral and written, in which emphasis stressed issues of sanctification of the life of Israel, the people, in the aftermath of the destruction of the Temple of Jerusalem in A.D. 70.

The second set of the writings, 400-600, that culminated in the Bavli, stressed the dual issues of sanctification and also salvation, presenting a doctrine of Israel's redemption by the Messiah in the model of the sage himself. The amplification of the Mishnah, which led to the first of the two sets of writings, defined the literary expression of the theological program at hand. It begins with the Yerushalmi, addressed to the Mishnah as oral Torah. Alongside, work on the written Torah was carried on through Genesis Rabbah, a reading of the book of Genesis to interpret the history and salvation of Israel today in light of the history and salvation of the patriarchs and matriarchs of old, deemed to form the founders of the family of Israel after the flesh. A second important work, assigned to about the next half century, Leviticus Rabbah, ca. A.D. 450, read for the lessons of Israel's salvation the book of Leviticus, which stresses issues of the sanctification of Israel. So Leviticus was reread for its lessons of how Israel's sanctification in the here and now led to Israel's salvation at the end of time. Finally, the Bavli addressed both Torahs, oral and written, Mishnah and Scripture, within one and the same document — the first of the writings of the Judaism of the dual Torah to do so systematically and extensively. The difference between the Bavli and the earlier writings, therefore, is that while the authorship of the Yerushalmi systematically interpreted passages of the Mishnah, and the other documents, as is clear, did the same for books of the written Torah, the authorship of the Bavli did both. Alongside, there were some other treatments of biblical books important in synagogue liturgy, particularly the Five Scrolls, e.g., Lamentations Rabbati, Esther Rabbah, and the like. A remarkable compilation of scriptural lessons pertinent to the special occasions of the synagogue, Pesiqta deRab Kahana, reached closure at the same time — the fifth or sixth centuries — as well.

The difference in viewpoint between the documents from the Mishnah to the works on Leviticus, known as Sifra, and on Numbers and Deuteronomy, known as Sifré, is not merely technical. It is theological. The first of the two sets of writings, from the Mishnah to the Yerushalmi, exhibits no sign of interest in, or response to, the advent of Christianity. The second, from the Yerushalmi forward, lays points of stress and emphasis that, in retrospect, appear to respond to, and to counter, the challenge of Christianity. The point of difference, of course, is that from the beginning of the legalization of Christianity in the early fourth century, to the establishment of Christianity at the end of that same century, Jews in the Land of Israel found themselves facing a challenge that, prior to Constantine, they had found no compelling reason to consider. The specific crisis came when the Christians pointed to the success of the Church in the politics of the Roman state as evidence that Jesus Christ was king of the world, and that his claim to be Messiah and King of Israel had now found vindication. The Judaic documents that reached closure in the century after these events attended to questions of salvation, e.g., doctrine of history and of the Messiah, authority of the sages' reading of Scripture as against the Christians' interpretation, and the like, that had earlier not enjoyed extensive consideration.

IV. THE MISHNAH AND THE TALMUDS

Sages worked out in the pages of the Yerushalmi and, later on, the Bavli, as well

3

as in the exegetical compilations of the age a Judaism intersecting with the Mishnah's but essentially asymmetrical with it. The Talmuds and associated writings presented a system of salvation, but one focused on the salvific power of the sanctification of the holy people. The first of the two Talmuds, the one closed at the end of the fourth century, set the compass and locked it into place. The second concluded matters. The Mishnah, in ca. A.D. 200, described an orderly world, in which Israelite society is neatly divided among its castes, arranged in priority around the center that is the temple, systematically engaged in a life of sanctification remote from the disorderly events of the day. The two Talmuds portrayed matters quite differently. While the Talmuds aim principally at the exegesis and amplification of the laws of the Mishnah, they also point toward a matrix beyond the Mishnah's text. Transcending the Mishnah's facts, the Talmuds' authorships bring to the Mishnah a program defined outside of the Mishnah. The Talmuds' discussions, to begin with, are not limited to the contents of the Mishnah. Discourse encompasses a world of institutions, authorities, and effective power, quite beyond the imagination of the Mishnah's framers. The Talmuds' picture of that world, furthermore, essentially ignores the specifications, for these same matters, of the Mishnah's law.

To take one striking example, the Mishnah's government for Israel rests upon a high priest and a king, with administrative courts ascending upward to the authority of the Temple mount. The Talmuds do not even pretend that such a world exists, knowing in its place a set of small-claims courts and petty bureaus of state, over which rabbis, defined as judges, lawyers, and masters of disciples in the law, preside. At the head of it all is a patriarch, not a priest anointed for the purpose. That example provides an instance of the curious discontinuity between the Mishnah's view of the world and of the society of Israel, on the one side, and that of the Talmuds, continuous with the Mishnah and framed as little more than an exegesis of that code, on the other hand.

The Talmuds protrayed the chaos of Jews living among gentiles, governed by a diversity of authorities, lacking all order and arrangement, awaiting a time of salvation for which, through sanctification, they make themselves ready. That social fact of Israel's life did not change between 200 and 400 in the Land of Israel, and between 200 and 600 in Babylonia. But the representation of the social realities did change. The sages of both Talmuds represented themselves — and we have no reason to doubt them — as fully in charge of the everyday life of the community, hence in constant touch with a real "Israel" consisting of a social group living a palpable everyday life. We may compare the former authorship to legal philosophers, in abstract terms thinking about logic and order. The latter authorships, the ones of the Talmuds, encompassed men deeply involved in the administration of the concrete social group, "Israel" as a real-life community. We may see that authorships as analogous to judges, lawyers, bureaucrats, heads of local governments, not philosophers alone but men of affairs. When they represented "Israel," they drew upon concrete knowledge of, engagement in, a very real social world

4

indeed. The facts portrayed by this second authorship draw upon experience entirely beyond the imagination of the first one.

The Mishnah's Israel in imagination is governed by an Israelite king, high priest, and sanhedrin — a political world that for two centuries had existed, if at all, only in imagination or aspiration. The Talmuds' portrait of Israel represents Jews who lived under both rabbis near at hand, settling everyday disputes of streets and households, and also distant archons of a nameless state, to be manipulated and placated on earth as in heaven. The Mishnah's Judaism breathes the pure air of public piazza and stoa, the Talmuds', the ripe stench of private alleyway and courtyard. The image of the Mishnah's Judaism is evoked by the majestic Parthenon, perfect in all its proportions, conceived in a single moment of pure rationality. The Talmuds' Judaism is a scarcely-choate cathedral in process, the labor of many generations, each of its parts the conception of diverse moments of devotion, all of them the culmination of an on-going and evolving process of revelation in the here and now. The Mishnah's system presents a counterpart to Plato's *Republic* and Aristotle's *Politics*, a noble theory of it all. When we study the Mishnah, we contemplate a fine conception of nowhere in particular, addressed to whom it may concern, a utopian vision in an exact sense of the word. When we turn to the Talmuds, we see a familiar world, as we have known it from the Talmud's day to our own. It is a locative perspective upon the here and the now, so far as the Talmuds' portray that concrete present. In literary terms, in the transition from the Mishnah to the Talmuds we leave behind the strict and formal classicism of the Mishnah, like Plato's Republic describing for no one in particular an ideal society never, in its day, to be seen. We come, rather, to focus upon the disorderly detail of the workaday world, taking the utopian Mishnah along with us.

How precisely was the Mishnah studied in the two Talmuds? The answer to this question will prove critical in following the argument of Part Four of this book. It was, first, through line by line, word by word. The modes of study were mainly three. Sages asked about the meanings of words and phrases. Then they worked on the comparison of one set of laws with another, finding the underlying principles of each and comparing, and harmonizing, those principles. So they formed of the rather episodic rules a tight and large fabric. Third, they moved beyond the narrow limits of the Mishnah into still broader and more speculative areas of thought. Once the work of reading the new code got under way, an important problem demanded attention. What is the relationship between the Mishnah and the established Scripture of Israel, the written Torah? The Mishnah only occasionally adduces texts of the Scriptures in support of its rules. Its framers worked out their own topical program, only part of which intersects with that of the laws of the Pentateuch. They followed their own principles of organization and development. They wrote in their own kind of Hebrew, which is quite different from biblical Hebrew. So the question naturally arose, Can we through sheer logic discover the law? Or must we tease laws out of Scripture through commentary, through legal exegesis? Ther Mishnah represented an extreme in this debate, since, as I said, so many of its topics to begin with do not derive from Scripture, and, further, a large part of its laws ignores

5

Scripture's pertinent texts in that these texts are simply not cited. The two Talmuds therefore paid attention, also, to the relationship of the Mishnah to Scripture.

V. THE RELATION BETWEEN THE BAVLI AND YERUSHALMI

Each of the two Talmuds relates to the Mishnah. But both stand on their own. The Bavli is more than a secondary development of the Yerushalmi. On the one hand, both the Yerushalmi and the Bavli organize their materials as comments on Mishnah sentences or paragraphs. The two compositions, moreover, differ from all other documents of the rabbinic canon both in their focus — the Mishnah — and in their mode of discourse. That is to say, Mishnah exegesis and expansion find their place, in the entire corpus of rabbinic writings of late antiquity, solely in the two Talmuds. What is shared between the two Talmuds and the remainder of the canon deals with Scripture exegesis, on the one side, and deeds and sayings of sages, on the other. To give one simple example, while Leviticus Rabbah contains exegeses of Scripture found also in one or another of the two Talmuds, there is not a single passage of the Mishnah subjected, in Leviticus Rabbah, to modes of analysis commonplace in the two Talmuds, even though on rare occasion a Mishnah sentence or paragraph may find its way into Leviticus Rabbah. So the two Talmuds stand together as well as take up a position apart from the remainder of the canon. But while the two Talmuds treat the Mishnah paragraphs in the same order, they do not say the same thing about them. The two Talmuds treat the Mishnah paragraph in distinct and distinctive ways. They use different language to make their own points. Where they raise the same issue, it derives from the shared text, the Mishnah, and its logic. Both Talmuds respond to the Mishnah. But the Bavli does not depend overall on a conventional program supplied by the Yerushalmi. Even when the Yerushalmi and the Bavli share materials, the Bavli's use of those material does not depend upon the Yerushalmi's. Both refer back to the Mishnah and to the Tosefta, responding to the former in terms of the exegetical program precipitated by the contents available in the latter. When the two Talmuds wish to deal with the same issue, the overlap is in conception; but there is no point of verbal contact, let alone of intersection. Each Talmud undertakes its own analysis in its own way. Each Talmud bases its discussion on the common source (the Mishnah, sometimes also the Tosefta), but each one builds its discussion on the basis of points made by its selection of authorities and pursues matters in terms of its own established conventions of rhetoric. Occasionally, the Bavli's authorship draws upon a shared tradition, known also to the Yerushalmi's writers. But the point of interest of the Yerushalmi's writers commonly bears no relevance to the Bavli's authorship, which goes its own way. It remains to observe that the two Talmuds come into contact not only through shared access to the Mishnah and to the Tosefta as well as some materials of earlier authorities. The two Talmuds meet also in what appears to be a common exegetical program on questions or principles that bear upon a given Mishnah paragraph. But that common program derives over and over again from the contents of the Mishnah paragraph at hand, that is, the principles of law implied by a given rule. It may emerge from the overall task that, linking the Mishnah to

Scripture, formed the center of the hermeneutic labor of everyone who received the Mishnah and proposed to deal with it.

The Bavli and the Yerushalmi assuredly stand autonomous from one another. Each in its own way works out its own program of exegesis and amplification of the Mishnah. Word-for-word correspondences are few. Where materials are shared, moreover, they derive from either the Mishnah or the Tosefta or some antecedent convention of exegesis. But in all instances of shared language or conventional hermeneutics the framers of the Bavli worked things out on their own. They in no way accepted the Yerushalmi as a model for how they said things or for the bulk of what they said. What is shared, moreover, derives principally from the Mishnah. It comes, secondarily, from some sort of conventional program (partly encapsulated, also, in the Tosefta). But the Bavli's authors developed inherited intellectual conventions in a strikingly independent way.

On the other hand, the Bavli and the Yerushalmi most certainly do form a cogent part of a larger, continuous statement, that of "the one whole Torah of Moses, our rabbi" or, in modern theological language, Judaism. The two authorships wish to do much the same thing, which is to subject the Mishnah to a process of explanation and amplification. While the authors of the Bavli developed their own principles of hermeneutics, composition, and redaction, still, the upshot of their work, the Bavli as a whole, would not have baffled their predecessors, who created the Yerushalmi. Apart from disagreements on tertiary details, the two sets of authorities found themselves entirely at home in the conceptions, rhetoric, and documents created by their counterparts. That seems self-evident proof of the continuity of the Bavli with the Yerushalmi. But the continuity is because of the shared program of Mishnah-exegesis and amplification. For the Bavli flows not from the Yerushalmi but from the Mishnah. That is the source, also, of the Yerushalmi and hence the cause of the parallel course of both documents. At point after point, the two documents are connected not only to the common source but mainly or solely through that source. Where they go over the same problems, it is because the shared source presented these problems to the authors of both documents. In our comparison of the two documents, we found that the rhetoric and literary program of the Bavli owed remarkably little to those of its predecessor. It is a Mishnah paragraph or Tosefta passage that is held in common, on the one side, or a prior, severely abbreviated lemma of an earlier Amoraic authority, on the other. Where the two sets of authors deal with such a shared lemma, however, each group does exactly what it wishes, imputing words to the prior authority (as if the said authority had actually spoken those words) simply not known to the other group. More important, what the framers of the Bavli wished to do with a saying of an earlier Amoraic authority in no way responded to the policy or program of the Yerushalmi's authors. In no aspect did the Yerushalmi's interest in these shared sayings affect the Bavli's treatment of them. The point in common was that prior authorities explained the same passage of the Mishnah. From that simple starting point, the Bavli's authors went in a direction not imagined by the Yerushalmi's. The power and intellectual force of the Bavli's authors in that context vastly overshadowed the capacities of the Yerushalmi's. In one further point, the Bavli's authorship innovated, and that was in their capacity to read Scripture in that same systematic and purposive way in which they read the Mishnah. They furthermore composed large-scale treatments of scriptural passages much like those on Mishnah-paragraphs. The result was that through the medium of the Bavli Judaism would receive and read the written part of the Torah, or Scripture, in the same way as it received the oral part, or the Mishnah. That constituted the distinctive strength of the Bavli, and, in theological terms, accounts for its priority and authority in Judaism.

VI. THE TALMUD AND MIDRASH, HALAKHAH, AND AGGADAH

The preceding exposition has explained how the Bavli relates to Scripture, the Mishnah, the Tosefta, Yerushalmi, and related writings. It remains briefly to refer to some familiar terms concerning the Bavli. The first *halakhah*, a word that means law, how things are done. The second is *aggadah*, lore. The word comes from the root that, as a verb, yields "to tell, to report, to narrate," and, accordingly, *aggadah* commonly means narrative or story. It bears the secondary meaning of fable. The third is *Midrash*. The English word "exegesis" carries the same generic sense as the Hebrew word "Midrash." So far as the authorship of the Yerushalmi or the Bavli read and interpreted the Mishnah, they engaged in a process of *midrash*, and so too for Scripture. But the word midrash bears a more limited meaning, namely, interpretation for the purpose of discovering a pertinent rule (in the Mishnah) or theological truth (in Scripture).

Joined to the word *halakhah*, as in *midrash halakhah*, the word bears the meaning of deriving a rule or a law from a verse of Scripture. One important exercise is to show the relationship of a rule of the Mishnah to a statement found in Scripture, thus proving that the oral Torah restates principles sustained by the (now more authoritative) written Torah. Another exercise will derive from a verse of Scripture a rule not found in the Mishnah. The previously mentioned works, Sifra, to Leviticus, Sifré to Numbers, and the other Sifré, to Deuteronomy, all fall into the category of *midrash halakhah*. Joined to the word *aggadah*, that is, *midrash aggadah*, the word yields, "interpretation of a biblical story." Important parts of Genesis Rabbah and Leviticus Rabbah contain *midrash aggadah*, that is, amplifications of scriptural stories. The relationship of the Bavli, as a document, to these two genres of writing is simple. The Bavli's and Yerushalmi's authorships included sizable passages of both categories of writing, that is, *midrash halakhah* and also *midrash aggadah*. But while the Yerushalmi's authorship produced a major treatment of the Mishnah and only episodic statements focused upon Scripture, the Bavli's authorship, as is clear, built considerable systematic statements out of both types of writing, as it worked its way toward a massive and encyclopaedic restatement of both components of the Torah, written and oral.

VII. LITERATURE AND SOCIETY: THE CONTENTS OF THE TALMUD AND THE CONTEXT OF THE TALMUD

Since both Talmuds begin with the Mishnah, an account of the contents of each one must begin with a picture of the base-document. The Mishnah is a kind of law code, divided into six divisions, Agriculture, Seasons (holy days), Women (laws of the family, personal status, betrothal, marriage, divorce, also vows and some special problems), Damages (civil and criminal law, the organization and procedures of the courts), Holy Things (the temple, conduct of the sacrificial rites on an everyday basis, the upkeep of the temple buildings), and Purities (taboos affecting the temple cult, uncleanness in respect to persons). These six divisions viewed over all cover six principal topics: sanctification of the economy and support of the priesthood, the holy caste, sanctification of time, with reference to special occasions, appointed times and the Sabbath, sanctification of the family and the individual, the proper conduct of points of social conflict, the political life of the people, the sanctification of the Temple and its offerings, with special emphasis on the everyday and the routine occasions, and, finally, the protection of the Temple from uncleanness and the preservation of cultic cleanness. These six principal subjects form the center of the Mishnah's six divisions and, all together, cover the everyday life of the holy people in the here and now. Among the six divisions of the Mishnah, Yerushalmi addresses four, Agriculture, Women, Seasons, and Damages, and the Bavli treats four, Women, Seasons, Damages, and Holy Things.

The topical program throughout thus focuses upon the sanctification of the life of Israel, the Jewish people. The question taken up by the Mishnah, in the aftermath of the destruction of the Temple, is whether and how Israel is still holy. And the self-evidently valid answer is that Israel indeed is holy, and so far as the media of sanctification persist beyond the destruction of the holy place — and they do endure — the task of holy Israel is to continue to conduct that life of sanctification that had centered upon the Temple. Where now does holiness reside? It is in the life of the people, Israel — there above all. So the Mishnah may speak of the holiness of the Temple, but the premise is that the people — that kingdom of priests and holy people of Leviticus — constitutes the center and focus of the sacred. The land retains its holiness too, and in raising the crops, the farmer is expected to adhere to the rules of order and structure laid down in Leviticus, keeping each thing in its proper classification, observing the laws of the sabbatical year, for instance. The priesthood retains its holiness, even without the task of carrying out the sacrificial cult. Therefore priests must continue to observe the caste rules governing marriage, such as are specified in Leviticus.

Since the two Talmuds focus upon Seasons, Women, and Damages, let us address the main points important both to the Mishnah and the Talmuds in those divisions. These continue the special interest in sanctification. The relationship of man and wife forms a focus of sanctification, and that too retains its validity even now. The passage of time, from day to day with the climax at the Sabbath, from

9

week to week with the climax at the sanctification of the new month, from season to season with the climax at the holy seasons, in particular the first new moon after the atumnal equinox, marked by Tabernacles, and the first new moon after the vernal equinox, marked by Passover — these too continue to indicate the fundamental state and condition of Israel the people: all these modes of sanctification endure, surviving the destruction of the holy Temple.

Four of the six principal parts of the Mishnah deal with the cult and its officers. These are, first, Holy Things, which addresses the everyday conduct of the sacrificial cult; second, Purities, which takes up the protection of the cult from sources of uncleanness specified in the book of Leviticus (particularly Leviticus Chapters Twelve through Fifteen); third, Agriculture, which centers on the designation of portions of the crop for the use of the priesthood (and others in the same classification of a holy caste, such as the poor), and so provides for the support of the Temple staff; and, fourth, Appointed Times, the larger part of which concerns the conduct of the cult on such special occasions as the Day of Atonement, Passover, Tabernacles, and the like (and the rest of which concerns the conduct in the village on those same days, with the basic conception that what you do in the cult forms the mirror image of what you do in the village). Of these four parts, as we see, the Yerushalmi attends to three and the Bavli to three, both of them omitting Purities. Two further divisions of the document as a whole deal with every day affairs, one, Damages, concerning civil law and government, the other, Women, taking up issues of family, home, and personal status. That, sum and substance, is the program of the Mishnah. Both Talmuds take a keen interest in these divisions.

This account of the topical program of the two Talmuds — which themselves share the same points of emphasis — tells us what the Talmuds did with the received statement of the Mishnah. But, on their own, they made their powerful and original statements as well. The most important point of those statements was to shift the focus upon the Temple and its supernatural principles to close attention to the people Israel and its natural, this-worldly history. Once Israel, holy Israel, had come to form the counterpart to the Temple and its supernatural life, that other history — Israel's — would stand at the center of things. Accordingly, a new sort of memorable event came to the fore in the Talmud of the Land of Israel. It was the story of Israel's suffering, remembrance of that suffering, on the one side, and an effort to explain events of such tragedy, on the other. The components of the historical theory of Israel's sufferings were manifold. First and foremost, history taught moral lessons. Historical events entered into the construction of a teleology for the Yerushalmi's system of Judaism as a whole. What the law demanded reflected the consequences of wrongful action on the part of Israel. So, again, Israel's own deeds defined the events of history. But the paradox of the Talmuds' system lies in the fact that Israel can free itself of control by other nations only by humbly agreeing to accept God's rule. The nations — Rome, in the present instance — rest on one side of the balance, while God rests on the other. Israel must then choose between them. There is no such thing for Israel as freedom from both God and the nations, total autonomy and independence. There is only a choice of masters, a ruler on earth or a ruler in heaven. It is Israel's history that works out and expresses Israel's relationship with God. The critical dimension of Israel's life, therefore, is salvation, the definitive trait, a movement in time from now to then. It follows that the paramount and organizing category is history and its lessons. In the Talmuds we witness, among the Mishnah's heirs, a striking reversion to biblical convictions about the centrality of history in the definition of Israel's reality. The Bavli made the definitive statement of the matter. In the view expressed here, the principal result of Israel's loyal adherence to the Torah and its religious duties will be Israel's humble acceptance of God's rule. That humility, under all conditions, makes God love Israel.

> *"It was not because you were greater than any people that the Lord set his love upon you and chose you"* [Deut. 7:7]. The Holy One, blessed be he, said to Israel, "I love you because even when I bestow greatness upon you, you humble yourselves before me. I bestowed greatness upon Abraham, yet he said to me, *'I am but dust and ashes'* [Gen. 18:27]; upon Moses and Aaron, yet they said, *'But I am a worm and no man'* [Ps. 22:7]. But with the heathens it is not so. I bestowed greatness upon nimrod, and he said, *'Come, let us build us a city'* [Gen. 11:4]; upon Pharaoh, and he said, *'Who are they among all the gods of the countries?'* [2 Kings 18:35]; upon Nebuchadnezzar, and he said, *'I will ascend above the heights of the clouds'* [Isa. 14:14]; upon Hiram, king of Tyre, and he said, *'I sit in the seat of God, in the heart of the seas'* [Ezek. 28:2]"
>
> (B. Hullin 89a).

The heart of the matter then is Israel's subservience to God's will, as expressed in the Torah and embodied in the teachings and lives of the great sages. When Israel fully accepts God's rule, then the Messiah will come. Until Israel subjects itself to God's rule, the Jews will be subjugated to pagan domination. Since the condition of Israel governs, Israel itself holds the key to its own redemption. But this it can achieve only by throwing away the key. The paradox must be crystal clear: Israel acts to redeem itself through the opposite of self-determination, namely, by subjugating itself to God. Israel's power lies in its negation of power. Its destiny lies in giving up all pretense at deciding its own destiny. So weakness is the ultimate strength, forbearance the final act of self-assertion, passive resignation the sure step toward liberation. (The parallel for this paradox is in the person of the crucified Christ.) Israel's freedom is engraved on the tablets of the commandments of God: to be free is freely to obey. That is not the meaning associated with these words in the minds of others who, like the sages of the rabbinical canon, declared their view of what Israel must do to secure the coming of the Messiah.

VIII.   THE INFLUENCE AND SIGNIFICANCE OF THE TALMUD

The Bavli from its closure in the seventh century to the present formed the first and most important resources for study. One reason for the success of the Bavli, apart from its powerful representation of the unity of the Torah, written and oral, lay in the historical success of the Babylonian Jews as against the decline of the community in the Land of Israel. Islam centered on Babylonia, not on the Land of

Israel, and as the Islamic conquest of the Middle East, North Africa, and southern Europe took effect, the Jews of the West, as well as of the Middle East, looked to Babylonia for leadership. While one group of Jews, called Karaites, rejected the claim that God had revealed an oral Torah and therefore ignored both Talmuds, in the main, the Jews world over received the Bavli in precisely the terms in which it represented itself: the authoritative statement of the Torah, written and oral, of Sinai.

When Judaic authorities wished to study the Torah, they therefore devoted themselves to the Bavli, and, it follows, all authoritative statements within Judaism began with the Bavli, which defined the way of reading both Scripture and the Mishnah alike. To cite statements of that view: "It is virtually impossible to exaggerate the dominant position held by the Babylonian Talmud among Jews throughout the ages, so "Eliezer Berkovitz ("The Babylonian Talmud," *Encyclopaedia Judaica* [Jerusalem, 1971: Macmillan], p. 767). "What the Bible had meant for Talmudic civilization, the [Babylonian] Talmud now meant for medieval Jewish life," writes Gerson D. Cohen. He says, "Medieval Judaism thus became synonymous with the law of the Babylonian Talmud." ("The Talmudic Age," in Leo W. Schwarz, ed; *Great Ages and Ideas of the Jewish People* [New York, 1956: Random House], p. 210). Today, the Talmud, meaning the one of Babylonia, serves as a principal resource of Reform and Reconstructionist Judaism, while both Conservative and Orthodox authorities continue to identify Judaism with the Bavli. According to the Israeli Talmudist, Adin Steinsaltz, "If the Bible is the cornerstone of Judaism, then the [Babylonian] Talmud is the central pillar, soaring up from the foundations and supporting the entire spiritual and intellectual edifice. In many ways the [Babylonian] Talmud is the most important book in Jewish culture, the backbone of creativity and national life. No other work has had a comparable influence on the theory and practice of Jewish life, shaping spiritual content and serving as a guide to conduct. The Jewish people have always been keenly aware that their continued survival and development depend on the study of the [Babylonian] Talmud (*The Essential Talmud*, Chaya Galai, trans. [New York, 1976: Bantam], p. 3). These and other statements demonstrate the centrality of the Bavli for Judaism. They justify my repeated resort to traits of the Bavli in the description, analysis, and interpretation of Judaism, as well as in the comparison of Judaism to Christianity.

CHAPTER TWO
THE SAGE, MIRACLE, AND MAGIC

I. THE CONVENTIONAL DISTINCTION BETWEEN MIRACLE AND MAGIC, AND ITS RELEVANCE TO THE DIFFERENCE BETWEEN SCIENCE AND MAGIC

The Christian Gospels, both canonical and otherwise, persistently represented Jesus Christ as a miracle-worker. They furthermore differentiated between miracles, which Jesus accomplished, and magic. The stories about sages presented in the canonical writings of the Judaism of the dual Torah present sages as miracle-workers and make the same important distinction. We may therefore establish an important trait shared by the writings of the two religious traditions, and, in this chapter, we see how the sage is represented as a miracle-worker. That evidence then validates the claim that the Judaism of the dual Torah had access to the same type of story that, in the hands of the authors of the Christian gospels, formed the centerpiece of stories about the life of Christ[2].

The received definition of the difference between miracle and magic, long familiar in history of religion, allows us to differentiate, also, between science and magic. The difference, many have maintained, is conventional. It is that, in any given system, people know the difference between acts of religion, that is, miracles, and those of superstition, namely, magic by reference to the source and standing of the one who does a deed deemed out of the ordinary. The extraordinary deeds the true God (or the agents thereof, that is, angels or holy persons) does are miracles. The extraordinary deeds a false god (with the same qualification) does are magic. The difference then is social and systemic, the distinction merely a conventional usage of society. The distinction makes a difference, in particular, in exchanges between systems, e.g., Elijah and the prophets of Baal. It connotes the simple judgment that what my side does is a miracle; and by the way, it works; what your side does is magic, whether or not it works. The possibility of communication between systems concerning wonders or unusual events rests upon the distinction at hand.

That definition, from a theoretical perspective bordering on the nihilistic to be sure, derives merely from conventional usage. But the distinction allows us to assess whether or not there is any difference between religion and magic. For — in the nature of things — the convention is imputed and alleged, subject to inductive inquiry and empirical testing, not explicit in the statements of a given system. An outside party sorts matters out by appealing to the (self-evident) convention at hand, which — by the way — participants or native-speakers also will make explicit. A participant will repeat the distinction in full credence. Validating the distinction

---

[2]I originally prepared this lecture for a conference at Brown University, August 9-13, 1987, on religion and science, religion and magic. I then put it aside in favor of a different problem for the same conference,

requires us to demonstrate, in a series of cases, that the same merely conventional and wholly extrinsic difference applies throughout. It is a distinction based on no more subtle an indicator than the recognition that what is in is in, and the out, also, is out. We can identify a variety of cases for study of whether the imputed distinction also is implicit (since it never is explicit) and therefore valid.

That observation brings us to the issue of magic and science. My thesis is that the same distinction applies, and that the difference in any setting between what is deemed magic and what is deemed science or learning derives from the larger setting in which people know the one from the other. A given system has no difficulty in conceding that the rules that apply within apply also without; prophecy exists in Israel and the nations, and so too sagacity (to refer to the case at hand). The ins have science, so do the outsiders. But the science of the insiders, of the system, is true. The science of the outsiders is (mere) magic. Rationality begins, then, in the mind of the one who imputes to a given mode of thought the status of rationality. My thesis, then, is that if we wish to ask whether and how a given system of knowledge distinguishes between learning of one sort and that of some other, we may be wise to begin with the same distinction based upon an appeal to the definitive traits of a given social and cultural system. That is to say, under any given circumstance, the indicator is systemic and derives from the social world beyond itself. To state matters simply, science is what I know, magic is what you know. True, I too may know magic; but you can never know science.

We then seek a case, proposing on the basis of a single instance a plausible rule for further testing. Our selection of an appropriate case finds guidance in the simple and conventional view just now cited. Can we identify a case in which, it is clear, a system differentiates between scientific learning and magical learning, and, furthermore, tells us what difference the difference makes? If we simply begin with the stipulated notion that the distinction between learning and magic is possible and ask whether we can identify a case in which such a (theoretical) distinction clearly is in play, we may progress toward the working hypothesis on the matter that I have proposed: the systemic centrality of decisions on what is science or learning, what is magic. How we know we have such a case requires specification. The answer will have to be explicit in the details of the proposed case. We shall know that the details do make such a distinction explicit by analogy to the distinction already established, the one between miracle and magic. What I do is a miracle, what you do is a magic. Can we move that same (conventional, theoretically-impoverished but therefore unencumbered) definition from one realm to the other, from religion ro science or learning? It will yield as criterion for a pertinent case the trait of mind that holds this: what I know is science, what you know is magic. Indeed so, because the same stories that tell me the difference between magic and miracle also persuade me of the distinction between magic and science or rationality or learning (in this context, the three are not to be distinguished).

14

Let me unpack this simple crition. If we ask whether we can distinguish in any terms scientific or rational learning from magical or other-than-rational learning, the answer will derive to begin with from a case in which, so far as the conventional distinction is concerned, we are able to find in operation precisely such a distinction. To state matters with emphasis: *What we require, in concrete terms, is a case in which a system explicitly makes the distinction itself—and makes clear that the distinction makes a difference.* And we shall see that in every case in the religious framework under discussion, the distinction between miracle and magic and the distinction between science and magic is precisely the same. In both cases the distinction flows from the system's larger systemic judgment on who and what are inside, who and what are outside. A given system knows the difference because of its deeper judgment upon its own social limits. And, it will follow (for the purposes of offering a hypothesis for testing in other cases), the distinction between magic and learning derives from the same systemic, that is, socially-conventional, sources as the one between magic and miracle.

I may therefore define a useful experiment in identification of appropriate evidence and analysis of that evidence. I frame the question as in parallel components: is it the case that, [1] just as people appeal to (mere, self-evident) truth, which is to say, the received and established convention of knowledge put forth by their own group, for distinguishing miracle from magic, so, [2] in the same way, they know the difference between science or learning and magic? Whether or not there is a perceived difference between science and magic, and if there is, whether the difference bears important consequences (even of a conventional character) now remains to be determined. We seek a specific case in which science differs from magic — and in which the difference is not implicit, awaiting our recognition of a category long-missed, but entirely explicit.

II. THE RELEVANCE OF A JUDAISM TO DISCOVERING THE DISTINC-TION BETWEEN LEARNING AND MAGIC

I draw my case from a particular Judaism. To begin with, therefore, let me explain why a Judaism is pertinent to the issue at hand. The reason for the relevance of any Judaism derives from the character of the Torah, only secondarily from that of the Judaism of the dual Torah which I shall discuss presently. Any Judaic religious system will prove particularly relevant to the issue of a distinction between learning and magic. The reason is simple. It is a basic and indicative trait of every Judaism, appealing as all of them do to the Hebrew Scriptures, and, in particular, to the Pentateuch as God's revelation at Sinai, that God has a will for Israel. That will — the Torah, or revelation — takes the particular form of knowledge, encompassing science even in our limited American sense, which in revelation, or the Torah, God has handed over to Israel. Since any Judaism takes as the core of revelation the notion that there is knowledge that derives from God, it must follow that a theory of both knowledge or science and magic may be expected to emerge. A religion in which what God had to say did not take the form of science or knowledge would

15

prove a less likely arena for inquiry. How so? The very content of the Torah is extensive knowledge of matters of science, for example, cosmology and cosmogony, the nature of the universe, the origins of the world of nature, social science, for instance, matters of the social rules of society, the laws of history and the origins and workings of culture, the history of humanity, and the like. I need not appeal solely to the contents of the Pentateuch. Quite to the contrary, diverse Judaisms and Christianities, appealing to that document, find in it important scientific knowledge. That is why I think we may turn to a Judaism for a test-case of whether people differentiate between science or systematic learning, on the one side, and magic and magical learning on the other — differentiate as to the character of learning vs. magic, the source of learning vs. the source of magic, and the validating criteria of the one as against the other.

Anyone who doubts that the content of the Torah encompasses the entire realm of science and learning need only study the history of how Scripture formed an obstacle impeding the development of a vast range of natural sciences, whether botany, biology, geology, physics, and also of social sciences and humanities, such as linguistics, ethnography, a broad range of historical studies, anthropology, and on and on. Until the diverse secular sciences (now using the word in the broader sense of systematic knowledge or learning) could free themselves of the thrall of the Hebrew Scriptures, learning as we now know it was not possible. That fact — the history of the natural and social sciences and a large sector of the humanities in the West and in modern times — proves the simple proposition that the contents of the Torah, that is, God's will, constitute scientific learning. We therefore have reason to expect a religion that imputes to God a corpus of scientific learning to distinguish between learning and magic, just as a religious system — it is generally conceded — can tell the difference between miracle and magic — even if only on a conventional basis. Having established the relevance of Scripture to our analysis of any Judaism, let me turn to the specific lesson that Scripture will have taught to the framers of any Judaic system that cared to listen.

III. EXPLICIT RECOGNITION IN SCRIPTURE OF THE DIFFERENCE BETWEEN SCIENCE AND MAGIC: THE CASE OF THE MAGICIANS OF PHARAOH IN SCRIPTURE

Since all Judaisms appeal to Scripture, let me begin the argument by a simple demonstration that Scripture itself recognizes the distinction between learning and. magic. That briefly-stated proof will establish the relevance of the case at hand and permit us to move directly to the center of my argument. We do indeed have a case in which Scripture itself, which identifies as well-equipped sages figures who in learning and in deed confront Israelite sages. These are the magicians of Pharaoh, who know how to do precisely what Moses does, and who do it: Israel's learning and deed in confrontation with the other's learning and deed. Let me now present

---

[1] I reproduce the translation *Tanakh. A New Translation of the Holy Scriptures According to the Traditional Hebrew Text* (Philadelphia, N.Y., Jerusalem, 1985: The Jewish Publication Society).

the pertinent passages. and point to the facts that all scriptural systems will have inherited from them[3]:

> The Lord said to Moses and Aaron, "When Pharaoh speaks to you and says, 'Produce your marvel,' you shall say to Aaron, 'Take your rod and cast it down before Pharaoh.' It shall turn into a serpent...Aaron cast down his rod in the presence of Pharaoh and his courtiers, and it turned into a serpent. Then Pharaoh, for his part, summoned the wise men and the sorcerers, and the Egyptian magicians, in turjn, did the same with their spells; each cast down his rod, and they turned into serpents. But Aaron's rod swallowed their rods.
>
> Ex. 7:8-12

> And the Lord said to Moses, "Say to Aaron: Take your rod and hold out your arm over the waters of Egypt...that they may turn to blood...." But when the Egyptian magicians did the same with their spells, Pharaoh's heart stiffened, and he did not heed them.
>
> Ex. 7:19-22

> And the Lord say to Moses, "Say to Aaron: Hold out your arm with the rod over the wivers...and bring up the frogs on the land of Egypt." Aaron held out his arm...and the frogs came up and covered the land of Egytp. But the magicians did the same with their spells, and brought frogs upon the land of Egypt.
>
> Ex. 8:1-3

> Then the Lord said to Moses, "Say to Aaron: Hold out your rod and strike the dust of the earth, and it shall turn to live throughout the land of Egypt."...The magicians did the like with their spells to produce lice, but they could not. The vermin remained upon man and beast; and the magicians said to Pharaoh, "This is the finger of God!"
>
> Ex. 8:12-15

> Then the Lord said to Moses and Aaron, "Each of you take handfuls of soot from the kiln, and let Moses throw it toward the sky in the sight of Pharaoh. It shall become a fine dust all over the land of Egypt and cause an inflammation breaking out in boils on man and beast throughout the land of Egypt." So they took soot of the kiln and appeared before Pharaoh...The magicians were unable to confront Moses because of the inflammation, for the inflammation afflicted the magificians as well as all the other Egyptians...
>
> Ex. 9:8-11

Treating the narrative as unitary, we may say that, at this point, the magicians of Egypt are removed from the scene; twice they did what Moses did, twice they failed to do so. The text as we receive it — and therefore as it will have been read by the sages of late antiquity who produced the canon of the Judaism of the dual Torah — makes these points.

[1] The Egyptian "magicians" can do some things that Moses and Aaron do.
[2] Therefore their knowledge yields precisely the kinds of wonders that Moses and Aaron are able to accomplish.

17

[3] But the Egyptian "magicians" cannot do some of the things that Moses and Aaron can do.

[4] So their knowledge is not so effective as that of Moses and Aaron.

The stories therefore contain that implicit distinction that precipitates our inquiry. Moses and Aaron are not called magicians, but they do the things that magicians do. So they are comparable — but different. How are they different, and how do we know the difference? We moreover have knowledge of two kinds, the one of the insider, the other of the outsider. The knowledge produces the capacity to do wonders, whether we call them miraculous or magical acts. The distinctions between "our" knowledge and "theirs" are implicit.

IV. THE WONDERING-WORKING PHILOSOPHERS OF FORMATIVE JUDAISM, THEIR SCIENCE AND THEIR MIRACLES

My argument to this point is that if we wish to know how a system distinguishes science from magic, miracle from magic, we do well to follow the way in which a system that, in its very definition and essence appeals to science and moreover establishes the distinction between science and magic, knows the difference. There are two points at stake.

[1] In line with the conventional distinction introduced before between miracle and magic, I have to insist that the difference be made explicit and objective (in the context of evidence), rather than allowed to surface out of our implicit reading of what texts really are supposedly saying.

[2] In line with my thesis, I have further to demonstrate that the same difference that separates miracle from magic also separates science from magic.

The literature of formative Judaism, which is the Judaism of the dual Torah, the canon of which was produced in the first seven centuries A.D. will present us with a case in which [1] people make an explicit distinction between miracle and magic, [2] in which they further distinguish science from magic, and in which [3] the difference in both cases is precisely the same. The Judaic (Israelite) sage, or rabbi, performs miracles and also masters the Torah, which is to say, all worthwhile science or learning. The gentile sage does magic and furthermore masters magic. Let me state with emphasis what is at stake in the analysis at hand:

The distinction between miracle and science, on the one side, and magic, on the other, derives from, and marks, the difference between Israel and the nations, which distinction flows — in both matters — from knowledge of the Torah of Moses, our Rabbi. What is at stake in the difference between learning and magic and between miracle and magic is always what is at stake in the system as a whole: the generative myth of the system in its endless ramifications and applications. Here as everywhere in a well-composed system, the details invariably repeat the message of the whole.

18

The general relevance of that particular period and religious system requires explanation. It derives from the peculiar character of the ideal type of that Judaism. The ideal-type is a sage, who bears the honorific title of rabbi. The sage is represented in the canonical writings of the Judaism of the dual Torah in two ways: he[4] is a master of learning, that is, science, and he also is a miracle-worker. The definition of a sage appealed, in particular, to the sage's knowledge of the Torah, thus to science, for reasons specified in sections ii and iii. At the same time, the sage had the power to do things other people could not do, hence miracles, supernatural actions, or magic (for our purpose, the choice of language does not matter). Since the sage is represented as both a man of learning in the Torah, and also as a man who can perform miracles, we have an ideal case for the study of how a system in a single uniform way differentiates learning from magic as it distinguishes miracles from magic[5]. By one and the same person, both distinctions will be required. This union in the sage of learning of a supernatural origin and power of a supernatural character explains why the sage provides us with a fine test-case for the theory I have proposed. If I can show that the representation of the sage in both aspects of his indicative traits — his mastery of truth, his capacity to interfer in the natural processes of the world — forms a cogent picture deriving from the generative problematic of the system embodied in the sage as an ideal-type, that is to say, a picture based upon the larger definitive traits of the Judaic system that defines, also, the sage, I shall have made my point for the case at hand[6]. Now to the case.

Who is defined as a sage? It is someone who has acquired knowledge that is in the status of the Torah, on the one side, and who has acquired that knowledge through discipleship to a prior sage, in particular. Because of the mode of acquisition, the sage takes his place in a direct line to Moses, called "our rabbi," and the sage hence has mastered the Torah revealed by God to Moses at Sinai. The principal religious authority of that Judaism, in its formative age therefore appeals for his own standing and status, as well as the standing and status of his science, to the myth of God's revelation, or Torah, reaching Israel, the Jewish people, in two media, was the sage. Since the definitive trait of the Judaic system at hand derives from the myth of the dual Torah, oral and written, revealed by God to Moses at Sinai, we see on the surface that the definition of learning and of miracles as distinct from charlatanism, quackery, or the black arts, and magic, derives from the larger system's prevailing generative myth and expresses in detail the main point of that myth.

---

[4]There is no woman-sage in the entire canon of the Judaism of the dual Torah in its formative stage.

[5]Admittedly, the case is ideal because its conditions meet the stipulations of the thesis at hand.

[6]It then becomes an interesting experiment to locate in other systems the distinction between the sage-scientist and the miracle-worker-saint, as against the charlatan-scientist and the maker of magic. When these are not one and the same (as a matter of the representation of ideal-types) then we face a fresh set of problems requiring attention.

19

The sage himself was represented as the embodiment of the Torah, and that meant what the sage knew and did was part of the revelation called the Torah. On that basis the sage not only could claim that what he knew was true, but also that what he did (out of the ordinary) was a miracle, just as what he did on an everyday basis was an exemplification of the rule of the Torah. In the figure of the sage, the Torah became incarnate; knowledge and miracles then coalesced. Let me spell out this point on the sage as the incarnation of the Torah and give examples of how it reaches expression, and we shall then turn to a concrete case in which the distinction between the knowledge of a sage and the knowledge of an outsider ("magician") is drawn. Both God's will in Heaven and the sage's words on earth constituted Torah.

The claim that a sage himself was equivalent to a scroll of the Torah — a material, legal comparison, not merely a symbolic metaphor is expressed in the following legal thus practical rules, deriving from the Yerushalmi (Talmud of the Land of Israel):

A.   He who sees a disciple of a sage who has died is as if he sees a scroll of the Torah that has been burned.

Y. Moed Qatan 3:7.X.

I.   R. Jacob bar Abayye in the name of R. Aha: "An elder who forgot his learning because of some accident which happened to him — they treat him with the sanctity owed to an ark [of the Torah]."

Y. Moed Qatan 3:1.XI.

The sage therefore is represented as equivalent to the scroll of the Torah, and, turning the statement around, the scroll of the Torah is realized in the person of the sage. The conception is not merely figurative or metaphorical, for, in both instances, actual behavior was affected.

Still more to the point, what the sage did had the status of law; the sage was the model of the law, thus once again enjoyed the standing of the human embodiment of the Torah. Since the sage exercised supernatural power as a kind of living Torah, his very deeds served to reveal law, as much as his word expressed revelation. That is a formidable component of the argument that the sage embodied the Torah, another way of saying that the Torah was incarnated in the person of the sage. The capacity of the sage himself to participate in the process of revelation is illustrated in two types of materials. First of all, tales told about rabbis' behavior on specific occasions immediately are translated into rules for the entire community to keep. Accordingly, he was a source not merely of good example but of prescriptive law. Here is a sequence of rather trivial instances of how a sage's deed constituted a Torah-law, that is, a valid precedent:

X.   R. Aha went to Emmaus, and he ate dumpling [prepared by Samaritans].
Y.   R. Jeremiah ate leavened bread prepared by them.
Z.   R. Hezekiah ate their locusts prepared by them.
AA. R. Abbahu prohibited Israelite use of wine prepared by them.

Y. Abodah Zarah 5:4:III

These reports of what rabbis had done enjoyed the same authority, as statements of the law on eating what Samaritans cooked, as did citations of traditions in the names of the great authorities of old or of the day. What someone did served as a norm, if the person was a sage of sufficient standing.

Far more common in the Talmud are instances in which the deed of a rabbi is adduced as an authoritative precedent for the law under discussion. It was everywhere taken for granted that what a rabbi did, he did because of his mastery of the law. A deed is a valid precedent because of the source of the knowledge of the person who does the deed. Even though a formulation of the law was not in hand, a tale about what a rabbi actually did constituted adequate evidence on how to formulate the law itself. So from the practice of an authority, a law might be framed quite independent of the person of the sage. The sage then functioned as a lawgiver, like Moses. Among many instances of that mode of generating law are the following.

A. Gamaliel Zuga was walking along, leaning on the shoulder of R. Simeon b. Laqish. They came across an image.
B. He said to him, "What is the law as to passing before it?"
C. He said to him, "Pass before it, but close [your] eyes."
D. R. Isaac was walking along, leaning on the shoulder of R. Yohanan. They came across an idol before the council building.
E. He said to him, "What is the law as to passing before it?"
F. He said to him, "Pass before it, but close [your] eyes."
G. R. Jacob bar Idi was walking along, leaning upon R. Joshua b. Levi. They came across a procession in which an idol was carried. He said to him, "Nahum, the most holy man, passed before this idol, and will you not pass by it? Pass before it but close your eyes."

Y. Abodah Zarah 3:11.II.

The example of a rabbi served to teach how one should live a truly holy life. The requirements went far beyond the measure of the law, extending to refraining from deeds of a most commonplace sort. The example of rabbinical virtue, moreover, was adduced explicitly to account for the supernatural or magical power of a rabbi. There was no doubt, in people's imagination, therefore, that the reason rabbis could do the amazing things people said they did was that they embodied the law and exercised its supernatural or magical power. This is stated quite openly in what follows.

C. There was a house that was about to collapse over there [in Babylonia], and Rab set one of his disciples in the house, until they had cleared out everything from the house. When the disciple left the house, the house collapsed.
D. And there are those who say that it was R. Adda bar Ahwah.
E. Sages sent and said to him, "What sort of good deeds are to your credit [that you have that much merit]?"
F. He said to them, "In my whole life no man ever got to the synagogue in the morning before I did. I never left anybody there when I went out. I never

21

walked four cubits without speaking words of Torah. Nor did I ever mention teachings of Torah in an inappropriate setting. I never laid out a bed and slept for a regular period of time. I never took great strides among the associates. I never called my fellow by a nickname. I never rejoiced in the embarrassment of my fellow. I never cursed my fellow when I was lying by myself in bed. I never walked over in the marketplace to someone who owed me money.

G. "In my entire life I never lost my temper in my household."

H. This was meant to carry out that which is stated as follows: "I will give heed to the way that is blameless. Oh when wilt thou come to me? I will walk with integrity of heart within my house" (Ps. 101:2).

Y. Taanit 3:11.IV.

The correlation between learning and teaching, on the one side, and supernatural power or recognition, on the other, is explicit in the following.

A. R. Yosa fasted eighty fasts in order to see R. Hiyya the Elder [in a dream]. He finally saw him, and his hands trembled and his eyes grew dim.

B. Now if you say that R. Yosa was an unimportant man, [and so was unworthy of such a vision, that is not the case]. For a weaver came before R. Yohanan. He said to him, "I saw in my dream that the heaven fell, and one of your disciples was holding it up."

C. He said to him, "Will you know him [when you see him]?"

D. He said to him, "When I see him, I shall know him." Than all of his disciples passed before him, and he recognized R. Yosa.

E. R. Simeon b. Laqish fasted three hundred fasts in order to have a vision of R. Hiyya the Elder, but he did not see him.

F. Finally he began to be distressed about the matter. He said, "Did he labor in learning of Torah more than I?"

G. They said to him, "He brought Torah to the people of Israel to a greater extent than you have, and not only so, but he even went into exile [to teach on a wider front]."

H. He said to them, "And did I not go into exile too?"

I. They said to him, "You went into exile only to learn, but he went into exile to teach others."

Y. Ketubot 12:3.VII.

This story shows that the storyteller regarded as a fact of life the correlation between mastery of Torah sayings and supernatural power — visions of the deceased, in this case. That is why Simeon b. Laqish complained, EF, that he had learned as much Torah as the other, and so had every right to be able to conjure the dead. The greater supernatural power of the other then was explained in terms of the latter's superior service to "Torah." It seems to me pointless to distinguish supernatural power from magic. The upshot is that the sage was made a magician by Torah learning and could save Israel through Torah, source of the most powerful magic of all. That explains why the respect paid to the Torah also was due to the sage, a view quite natural in light of the established identification of sage and Torah.

Accordingly, what a sage says is treated precisely as statements in Scripture and the Mishnah are received. That is to say, the same modes of exegetical inquiry pertaining to the Mishnah and Scripture apply without variation to statements made by rabbis of the contemporary period themselves. Indeed, precisely the same theological and exegetical considerations come to bear both upon the Mishnah's statements and opinions expressed by talmudic rabbis. Since these were not to be distinguished from one another in the requirement that opinion be suitably grounded in Scripture, they also should be understood to have formed part of precisely the same corpus of Torah truths. What the Mishnah and the later rabbi said expressed precisely the same kind of truth: revelation — whether through the medium of Scripture, or that contained in the Mishnah, or that given in the opinion of the sage himself. The way in which this search for proof texts applies equally to the Mishnah and to the rabbi's opinion is illustrated in the following passage.

A. The party of Korah has no portion in the world to come, and will not live in the world to come [Mishnah Sanhedrin 10:4].

B. What is the scriptural basis for this view?

C. "So they and all that belonged to them went down alive into Sheol; and the earth closed over them, and they perished from the midst of the assembly" (Num. 16:33).

D. "The earth closed over them" — in this world.

E. "And they perished from the midst of the assembly" — in the world to come [Mishnah Sanhedrin 10:4D-F].

F. It was taught: R. Judah b. Batera says, "The contrary view is to be derived from the implication of the following verse:

G. "'I have gone astray like a lost sheep; seek thy servant and do not forget they commandments' (Ps. 119:176).

H. "Just as the lost object which is mentioned later on in the end is going to be searched for, so the lost object which is stated herein is destined to be searched for" [Tosefta Sanhedrin 13:9].

I. Who will pray for them?

J. R. Samuel bar Nahman said, "Moses will pray for them.

K. [This is proved from the following verse:] "'Let Reuben live, and not die, [nor let his men be few]' (Deut. 33:6)."

L. R. Joshua b. Levi said, "Hannah will pray for them."

M. This is the view of R. Joshua b. Levi, for R. Joshua b. Levi said, "Thus did the party of Korah sink ever downward, until Hannah went and prayed for them and said, 'The Lord kills and brings to life; he brings down to Sheol and raises up' (1 Sam. 2:6)."

Yerushalmi Sanhedrin 10:4.I.

We have a striking sequence of proof texts, serving (1) the cited statement of the Mishnah, A-C, then (2) an opinion of a rabbi in the Tosefta, F-H, then (3) the position of a rabbi, J-K and L-M. The process of providing proof texts therefore is central; the nature of the passages requiring the proof texts, a matter of indifference. We see that the search for appropriate verses of Scripture vastly transcends the purpose of studying the Mishnah and Scripture, the exegesis of their rules, or the provision of adequate authority for the Mishnah and its laws. In fact, any proposition that is to be taken seriously, whether in the Mishnah, in the Tosefta, or in the mouth of a talmudic sage himself, will elicit interest in scriptural support. Distinctions are not made among media — (1) oral, (2) written, or (3) living — of the Torah. The Torah — in our language, the canon of revealed truth — is in three media, not two. Scripture, the Mishnah, the sage — the three spoke with equal authority. While the canon was in three parts — Scripture, Mishnah, sage — the sage, in his authoritative knowledge of what the other parts meant and in embodying that meaning in his life and thought, took primacy of place. This fact will form the centerpiece of the argument of Chapter Three.

V. EXPLICIT RECOGNITION IN CANONICAL WRITINGS OF FORMATIVE JUDAISM THAT BOTH THE ISRAELITE SAGE AND THE GENTILE MASTER THE SAME SCIENCE AND ART

Just as Aaron and Moses and the Egyptian magicians share the same knowledge, with the science of the former superior to that of the latter, so we can show that in the Judaism of the dual Torah, people imputed to gentiles the mastery of power in both science and wonder-working. The difference, then, between Israelite and gentile power, assigning to the former science and miracle, to the latter, mere magic (in the media of both learning and doing), does not derive from qualities intrinsic to what is known or done, rather to the one who knows and does. That then underlines the systemic origin of the distinctions, wherever drawn. The canonical authorship had no difficulty, in reading the story of Pharaoh's magicians, in believing they had magical knowledge and power:

A. "Then the magicians said to Pharaoh, 'This is the finger of God'" (Ex. 8:19):

B. [Since the reference is to the creation of lice, which the Egyptian magicians did not know how to make,] said R. Eleazar, "On the basis of that statement we learn that a demon cannot make a creature smaller than a barley seed..."

E. Said Rab to R. Hiyya, "I myself saw a Tai-Arab take a sword and chop up a camel, then ring a bell and the camel arose."

F. He said to him, After this was there blood or dung? If not, it was merely an illusion."

b. San. 67b/M. San. 7:11.VIII

The gentile knows what the Israelite knows. But Aaron and Moses are God's messengers, and the gentile magician is a demon. The difference between miracle and magic and between science and magic is one and the same, namely, (in somewhat jarring language) the source of the accreditation of the scientist. There is, then, no intrinsic difference between Israelite science and gentile science, Israelite wonder-working and gentile wonder-working. The extrinsic difference is God's sponsorship of the former, the demonic character of the latter, or, in secular terms, one is ours, the other is theirs, and that without regard to whether we deal with knowledge or action. The distinction is systemic, and the difference is social and conventional. Here is yet another story in which the story-teller explicitly denies a difference between a sage's knowledge and miracle working and a gentile woman's knowledge and magic. They are consubstantial in all details:

24

A. Yannai came to an inn. He said to them, "Give me some water to drink." They brought him a flour-and-water drink.

B. He saw that the woman's lips were moving. He poured out a little of the drink and it had turned into scorpions. He said to her, "I drank something of yours, now you drink something of mine."

C.q He gave her something to drink, and she turned into an ass. He mounted her and rode her out into the market place.

D. Her girl-friend came and nullified the charm, so he was seen riding around in the market place on the back of a woman.

b. San. 67b/M. San. 7:11.IX

The upshot is just as before, though the story is considerably funnier. We know the difference between science and magic in the same way that we know the difference between miracle and magic: the point of origin.

VI. EXPLICIT RECOGNITION IN CANONICAL WRITINGS OF FORMATIVE JUDAISM OF THE DIFFERENCE BETWEEN SCIENCE AND MAGIC: THE CASE OF JOSEPH IN EGYPT

Joseph in Egypt provides yet another opportunity for observing the same insistence that on the basis of extrinsic traits we cannot differentiate the Israelite from the gentile magician, either as to knowledge or as to deed.

1. A. "The Lord was with Joseph, and he became a successful man; and he was in the house of his master, the Egyptian, and his master saw that the Lord was with him, and that the Lord caused all that he did to prosper in his hands" (Gen. 39:2-3):

B. R. Huna in the name of R. Aha: "[Joseph would go about] whispering [Torah-teachings] as he went in, whispering as he came out [praying for blessings], but in the end, he forgot: 'For God has made me forget all my toil' (Gen. 41:51).

C. "[Thinking that Joseph was a sorcerer,] his master would say to him, 'Mix me something hot,' and it came out mixed hot. 'Mix me something luke-warm,' and it came out lukewarm.

D. "He said to him, 'What is this, Joseph, straw to Ephron, pitchers to Kefar Hananiah, fleece to Damascus, witchcraft to Egypt?— witchcraft have you brought to the capital of witchcraft?'"

E. To what extent?

F. R. Huniah in the name of R. Aha, "It was to the extent that he saw the Presence of God hovering over him: 'and his master saw that the Lord was with him, and that the Lord caused all that he did to prosper in his hands. So Joseph found favor in his sight and attended him, and he made him overseer of his house and put him in charge of all that he had. From the time that he made him overseer in his house and of all that he had, the Lord blessed the Egyptian's house for Joseph's sake; the blessing of the Lord was upon all that he had in house and field' (Gen. 39:2-3)."

Genesis Rabbah LXXXVI:V

The presence of God is taken quite literally in the exposition at hand. Seeing Joseph whispering, the master thought he was practicing witchcraft, until he realized that it was God who did the wonders. The motif of the Egyptians' recognition of God is systematically introduced wherever appropriate. Joseph's remarkable knowledge in Egypt attests not to a detail — the difference between learning and magic — but to the system as a whole: God is the one true God.

VII. EXPLICIT RECOGNITION IN CANONICAL WRITINGS OF FORMATIVE JUDAISM OF THE DIFFERENCE BETWEEN SCIENCE AND MAGIC: THE CASE OF ISRAELITE AND GENTILE PROPHETS

The canonical documents we have surveyed one-sidedly attest to a single conviction: Israelite and gentile magicians practice the same magic. But one can differentiate the one from the other. Israelite and gentile sages know the same thing, which is to say, both derive their knowledge from God. But we can tell them apart. Israelite knowledge is direct, immediate, superior in origin — if not different in detail. The following exposition makes explicit the thesis I announced at the outset, which is that the same difference differentiates both between miracle and magic, and between science and magic. The difference is not intrinsic; we do not appeal to traits of Israelite wonder-working that tell us that, in its character, that wonder-working differs from its gentile counterpart. The stories we have examined insist on the opposite. The difference lies in God's differentiation between Israelite miracle and gentile magic, Israelite science and gentile magic. That is a theological formulation of the simple thesis that the insiders are in, and the outsiders, out. The explicit claim that gentile prophets have knowledge, which is to say, learning of divine origin (there being no other source of learning), but because of God's decision, it is inferior knowledge, follows:

1. A. "But God came to Abimelech in a dream by night [and said to him, 'Behold, you are a dead man, because of the woman whom you have taken, for she is a man's wife']" (Gen. 20:3):
   B. What is the difference between the prophets of Israel and those of the nations?
   C. R. Hama b. R. Haninah said, "The Holy One, blessed be he, is revealed to the prophets of the nations of the world only in partial speech, in line with the following verse of Scripture: 'And God called [WYQR, rather than WYQR' as at Lev. 1:1] Balaam' (Num. 23:16). [Lev. R. I:XIII.1.C adds: On the other hand, he reveals himself to the prophets of Israel in full and complete speech, as it is said, 'And the Lord called (WYR') to Moses' (Lev. 1:1).]"
   D. Said R. Issachar of Kepar Mandi, "[Lev. R. I:XIII.1.D adds: Should that prophecy, even in partial form, be paid to them as their wage? Surely not, in fact that is no form of speech to gentile prophets, who are frauds.] The connotation of the language, 'And God called to Balaam' (Num. 23:16) is solely unclean. That is in line with the usage in the following verse of Scripture: 'That is not clean, by that which happens by night' (Deut. 23:11). [So the root is the same, with the result that YQR at Num. 23:16 does not bear the meaning of God's calling to Balaam. God rather declares Balaam unclean.]"

26

    E. "But the prophets of Israel are addressed in language of holiness, purity, clarity, in language used by the ministering angels to praise God. That is in line with the following verse of Scripture: 'And they called one to another and said, "Holy, holy, holy is the Lord of hosts"' (Is. 6:3)."

2.   A. R. Yose said, "'The Lord is far from the evil, but the prayer of the righteous does he hear' (Prov. 5:29).

    B. "'The Lord is far from the wicked' refers to the prophets of the nations of the world.

    C. "'But the prayer of the righteous does he hear' refers to the prophets of Israel.

3.   A. R. Yose b. Bibah said, "The Holy One, blessed be he, appears to the prophets of the nations of the world only by night, when people take leave of one another: 'Now a word was secretly brought to me...at the time of leave-taking, from the visions of the night, when deep sleep falls on men' (Job 4:12-13)."

4.   A. Said R. Eleazar b. Menahem, "'The Lord is far from the evil' (Prov. 5:29) refers to the prophets of the nations of the world.

    B. "'But the prayer of the righteous does he hear' (Prov. 5:29) speaks of the prophets of Israel.

    C. "You furthermore find that the Holy One, blessed be he, appears to the prophets of the nations of the world only like a man who comes from some distant place. That is in line with the following verse of Scripture: 'From a distant land they have come to me, from Babylonia' (Is. 39:3).

    D. "But in the case of the prophets of Israel, he is always near at hand: 'And he appeared [not having come from a great distance]' (Gen. 18:1). 'And the Lord called' (Lev. 1:1).' [These usages bear the sense that he was right nearby.]"

5.   A. What is the difference between the prophets of Israel and those of the nations?

    B. R. Hinena said, "The matter may be compared to a king who, with his friend, was in a hall, with a curtain hanging down between them. When the king speaks to his friend, he turns back the curtain and speaks to his friend."

    C. And rabbis say, "The matter may be compared to the case of a king who had a wife and a concubine. When he walks about with his wife, he does so in full public view. When he walks about with his concubine, he does so discreetly. So too, the Holy One, blessed be he, is revealed to the prophets of the nations only at night,

    D. "in line with that which is written:' And God came to Balaam at night' (Num. 22:20). 'And God came to Laban the Aramean in a dream of the night' (Gen. 31:24). 'And God came to Abimelech in a dream by night' (Gen. 19:3)."

                          Genesis Rabbah LII:V.1-5

What captures the compositor-exegetes' attention is the statement that God communicated with Abimelech. This arouses their interest, since it would seem to imply that gentiles can receive God's word and become prophets. The upshot is a stunning statement that Israelite and gentile prophets differ not in what they know but in the way in which they know it. The same is so of miracle-workers/magicians: the Israelite differs from the gentile not in capacity but in authority and origin.

VIII.THE DISTINCTION BETWEEN LEARNING AND MAGIC IN FORMATIVE JUDAISM: A HYPOTHESIS BASED ON ONE CASE

The distinction between learning (inclusive of rationality or science) and magic emerges in the sources we have surveyed as essentially a convention of the system of the Judaism of the dual Torah. In still more explicit ways the canonical writings say the same thing about the distinction between miracle and magic. In both cases, therefore, the larger systemic program has defined the details represented by the matter at hand. The definition of miracle and Torah-learning derives from, and conforms to, the larger interests of the system and in detail expresses the system's main point. That result underlines the power of systematic thought to compose, whole and complete, a full account of all things, all together and all at once. The systemic disposition of any detail, even the important differentiations at hand, depends on the generative problematic — the urgent question — of the system-builders, and not on the intrinsic character of the evidence concerning either science or miracles.

Logic, the self-evidence of rationality of one sort rather than some other, the givenness of data, the importance and truth self-evidently inhering in one set of facts and lacking in another — these turn out to constitute conventions and only after the fact to form the systemic process and define its propositions. Since it is the fact that the system-builders' social (including political) circumstance defines the genera-tive problematic which imparts self-evidence to the systemically-definitive logic, if we wish to discover the origin of a system's understanding of the difference between science or learning and magic or between miracle and magic, we have in both matters to turn to the same inquiry for a single answer. It is, in my judgment, the context and circumstance of the system as a whole that will account, quite tangentially, also for the character of a system's sorting out knowledge, finding one sort valuable, another disreputable, and making sense of noteworthy events, deeming one sort miraculous, another sort magical.

The systemically-generative circumstance finds its definition in the out-there of the world in which the system-builders — and their imagined audience — flourish. Extraordinary political crises, on-going tensions of society, a religious crisis that challenges theological truth — these in time impose their definition upon thought, seizing the attention and focusing the concentration of the *systemopoieic* thinkers who propose to explain matters. Systems propose an orderly response to a disorderly situation, and that is their utility. Systems then come into existence at a point, and in a context, in which thoughtful people identify questions that cannot be avoided and must be solved. Such a circumstance, for the case at hand, emerges in the *polis*, that is, in the realm of politics and the context of persons in community, in the corporate society of shared discourse. The acute, *systemopoieic* question then derives from out-there, the system begins somewhere beyond the mind of the thoughtful intellects who build systems. Having ruled out the systemopoieic power of authors' or authorships' circumstance, therefore, I now invoke the *systemopoieic*

28

power of the political setting of the social group of which the system-builders form a part (in their own minds, the exemplification and realization).

Systemic logic enjoys self-evidence. But it is circumstance that dictates that absolute given, that sense of fittingness and irrefutable logic, that people find self-evident. System-building forms a symbolic transaction, and, by definition, represents symbol-change for the builders and their building. On the one hand, it is a social question that sets the terms and also the limits of the symbolic transaction, so symbol-change responds to social-change (at least for some). On the other hand, symbol-change so endures as to impose a new shape upon a social world.

But how shall we account for the origin of a system, including, of course, its important distinctions between acceptable and unacceptable knowledge? We can show correlation between a system and its circumstance, and, it must follow, between the internal logic of a system and the social givens in which the system flourishes. But correlation is not explanation. And the sources of explanation lie beyond the limits of cases, however many. The question facing system-builders carries with it one set of givens, not some other, one urgent and ineluctable question, which, by definition, excludes others. The context of the system-builders having framed the question before them, one set of issues, and not some other, issues of one type, rather than some other, predominate. Yet an element of a *priori* choice proves blatant. And that matter of selectivity points toward symbol-change as the prior, social change as the consequent, fact. Social change forms a necessary, but not sufficient, explanation.

When we point to the correlation between problem and program, context and contents, we do not explain matters. We only beg the question. True, the system-builders' social (including political) circumstance defines the generative problematic which imparts self-evidence to the systemically-definitive logic, encompassing its social component. But that important point of correspondence cannot by itself account in the end for the particular foci and the generative problematic of a system. I claim that a single political problem, a crisis that we can identify and describe, persuaded one group of the self-evidence of a given set of cogent truths, which yielded, for an author or authorship, the materials of a systematic rereading of all things in light of some one thing — thus, the documents that form the canon of that system. But that same circumstance did not impose upon another group in the same time, place, and situation, the same sense of the self-evidence of that system's matters identified as important and read in one way and not in some other. Different groups responded in diverse ways to the same crisis, which is proved by the fact that diverse systems, reaching documentary expression in canons of varying contents, did emerge from the same circumstances and did appeal to precisely the same foundation-document, the Hebrew Scriptures.

When therefore we appeal to the shared experience, hence social circumstance, to account for the power of self-evidence that lends strength to a system, holding together the system's identification of the urgent question with the obvious truth of the self-evident answer to that question, we prove our hypothesis by repeating it. And that tells us that we have come to the end of our inquiry. For the hypothesis may be illustrated, but not proved. The reason is that the hypothesis with which we conclude derives from our interpretation, specifically, of the correlation we observe between contents and context, circumstance and system, detail and main point. But that correlation does not encompass all of the systems that, in the same circumstance, we can imagine were taking shape. What we cannot do in this context is explain. That is, to account for the relationship between systemically definitive logic, which enjoys the standing of self-evident truth, and the context and circumstance in which a system originates and to which a system may be shown to respond, we must move beyond all our cases, all together. So when we move from description, analysis, and interpretation, to the larger matter of explanation, we complete the work that we can do, and that I set out to do. We come, however, not to an impasse but to a proper conclusion of a work correctly limited and appropriately defined. For the explanation of the whys and, especially, the wherefores of Judaic systems must derive from sources of theoretical thought other than the ones of (mere) description, analysis, and interpretation of Judaic texts in particular, or, even, of the facts of religion in general. But that impasse in finding the reason why need not impede our reaching one solid conclusion concerning systems and the symbolic transactions realized in them. *It is the priority of the social entity in systemic formation.* Or, to end where I began, the recognition that the distinctions important to a system, such as those I have traced, in the end constitute mere conventions of that system — hence of the society that the system serves in intellectual terms to realize.

CHAPTER THREE

THE UNWRITTEN GOSPELS OF JUDAISM:
STORIES TOLD BUT NOT COMPILED

I. THE THREE TYPES OF RECEIVED COMPOSITIONS, THE DUAL
    STRUCTURE OF THEIR ULTIMATE REDACTION

The final organizers of the Bavli, the Talmud of Babylonia, who, it is commonly alleged, flourished circa A.D. 500-600, had in hand a tripartite corpus of inherited materials awaiting composition into a final, closed document. First, the first type of material, in various states and stages of completion, addressed the Mishnah or took up the principles of laws that the Mishnah had originally brought to articulation. These the framers of the Bavli organized in accord with the order of those Mishnah-tractates that they selected for sustained attention. Second, they had in hand received materials, again in various conditions, pertinent to Scripture, both as Scripture related to the Mishnah and also as Scripture laid forth its own narratives. These they set forth as Scripture-commentary. In this way, the penultimate and ultimate redactors of the Bavli laid out a systematic presentation of the two Torahs, the oral, represented by the Mishnah, and the written, represented by Scripture. And, third, the framers of the Bavli also had in hand materials focused on sages. These in the received form, attested in the Bavli's pages, were framed around twin biographical principles, either as strings of stories about great sages of the past or as collections of sayings and comments drawn together solely because the same name stands behind all the collected sayings. These can easily have been composed into biographies. In the context of Christianity and of Judaism, it is appropriate to call the biography of a holy man or woman, meant to convey the divine message, a gospel[7]. Hence the question raised here: why no gospels in Judaism? The question is an appropriate one, because, as I shall show, there could have been. The final step — assembling available stories into a coherent narrative, with a beginning, middle, and end, for example — was not taken.

The Bavli as a whole lays itself out as a commentary to the Mishnah. So the framers wished us to think that whatever they wanted to tell us would take the form of Mishnah commentary. But a second glance indicates that the Bavli is made up of enormous composites, themselves closed prior to inclusion in the Bavli. Some of these composites — around 35% to 40% of Bavli's, if my sample is indicative[8]

---

[7] I use the word "gospel" with a small G as equivalent to "didactic life of a holy man, portraying the faith." Obviously, the Christian usage, with a capital G, must maintain that there can be a Gospel only about Jesus Christ. Claims of uniqueness are, of course, not subject to public discourse. In the present context, I could as well have referred to lives of saints, since Judaism of the dual Torah produced neither a gospel about a central figure nor lives of saints. Given the centrality of Moses "our rabbi," for example, we should have anticipated a "Gospel of Moses" parallel to the Gospels of Jesus Christ, and, lacking that, at least a "life of Aqiba," scholar, saint, martyr, parallel to the lives of various saints. We also have no autobiographies of any kind, beyond some "I"-stories, which themselves seem to me uncommon.

[8] I compared Bavli and Yerushalmi tractates Sukkah, Sanhedrin, and Sotah, showing the proportion of what I call Scripture-units of thought to Mishnah-units of thought. See my *Judaism. The Classic Statement. The Evidence of the Bavli* (Chicago, 1986: University of Chicago Press).

— were selected and arranged along lines dictated by a logic other than that deriving from the requirements of Mishnah commentary. The components of the canon of the Judaism of the dual Torah prior to the Bavli had encompassed amplifications of the Mishnah, in the Tosefta and in the Yerushalmi, as well as the same for Scripture, in such documents as Sifra to Leviticus, Sifré to Numbers, another Sifré, to Deuteronomy, Genesis Rabbah, Leviticus Rabbah, and the like. But there was no entire document, now extant, organized around the life and teachings of a particular sage. Even The Fathers According to Rabbi Nathan, which, as I shall show in Chapter Five, contains a good sample of stories about sages, is not so organized as to yield a life of a sage, or even a systematic biography of any kind. Where events in the lives of sages do occur, they are thematic and not biographical in organization, e.g., stories about the origins, as to Torah-study, of diverse sages; death-scenes of various sages. The sage as such, whether Aqiba or Yohanan ben Zakkai or Eliezer b. Hyrcanus, never in that document defines the appropriate organizing principle for sequences of stories or sayings. And there is no other in which the sage forms an organizing category for any material purpose[9].

Accordingly, the decision that the framers of the Bavli reached was to adopt the two redactional principles inherited from the antecedent century or so and to reject the one already rejected by their predecessors, even while honoring it. They organized the Bavli around the Mishnah. But they adapted and included vast tracts of antecedent materials organized as scriptural commentary. These they inserted whole and complete, not at all in response to the Mishnah's program. And, finally, while making provision for small-scale compositions built upon biographical principles, preserving both strings of sayings from a given master (and often a given tradent of a given master) as well as tales about authorities of the preceding half millennium, they never created redactional compositions, of a sizable order, that focused upon given authorities. But sufficient materials certainly lay at hand to allow doing so. In the three decisions, two of what to do and one of what not to do, the final compositors of the Bavli indicated what they proposed to accomplish: to give final form and fixed expression, through their categories of the organization of all knowledge, to the Torah as it had been known, sifted, searched, approved, and handed down, even from the remote past to their own day. So in our literary categories the compositors of the Bavli were encyclopaedists. Their creation turned out to be the encyclopaedia of Judaism, its summa, its point of final reference, its court of last appeal, its definition, it conclusion, its closure — so they thought, and so said those that followed, to this very day.

[9]The occasion, in the history of Judaism, at which biography defines a generative category of literature, therefore also of thought, will therefore prove noteworthy. The model of biography surely existed from the formation of the Pentateuch, with its lines of structure, from Exodus through Deuteronomy, set forth around the biography of Moses, birth, call, career, death. And other biographies did flourish prior to the Judaism of the dual Torah. Not only so, but the wall of the Dura synagogue highlights not the holy people so much as saints, such as Aaron and Moses. Accordingly, we must regard as noteworthy and requiring explanation the omission of biography from the literary genres of the canon of the Judaism of the dual Torah. One obvious shift is marked by Hasidism, with its special interest in stories about saints and in compiling those stories.

Shall we then draw so grand a conclusion from so modest a fact as how people sorted out available redactional categories[10]? Indeed so, if we realize that the modes by which thinkers organize knowledge leads us deep into the theses by which useful knowledge rises to the surface while what is irrelevant or unimportant or trivial sinks to the bottom. If we want to know what people thought and how they thought it, we can do worse than begin by asking about how they organized what they knew, on the one side, and about the choices they made in laying out the main lines of the structure of knowledge, on the other.

II. THE COMPOSITIONS NO ONE MADE: COLLECTIONS OF WISE SAYINGS AND BIOGRAPHIES

The Yerushalmi and the collections of scriptural exegeses comprise compositions made up of already-worked-out units of discourse focused upon the Mishnah and Scripture, respectively. Other completed units of thought, such as we might call paragraphs or even short chapters, deal with individual sages. Midrash-compilations and Mishnah-commentaries, both the Yerushalmi and the Bavli, contain a sizable quantity of sage units of discourse. These can surely have coalesced in yet a third type of book. Specifically, sayings and stories about sages could have been organized into collections of wise sayings attributed to various authorities (like Avot), on the one side, or sequences of tales, e.g., brief snippets of biographies or lives of the saints, on the other. Let me spell out what we do find, which will underline the noteworthy character of the fact at hand: materials not used for their obvious purpose, in the way in which materials of a parallel character were used for their purpose.

Let me define more fully the character of the discourse that focuses upon the sage. In this type of composition, e.g., a paragraph of thought, a story, things that a given authority said are strung together or tales about a given authority are told at some length. Whoever composed and preserved units of discourse on the Mishnah and on Scripture ultimately preserved in the two Talmuds did the same for the sage. What that fact means is simple. In the circles responsible for making up and writing down completed units of discourse, three distinct categories of interest defined the task: (1) exegesis of the Mishnah, (2) exegesis of Scripture, and (3) preservation and exegesis, in exactly the same reverential spirit, of the words and deeds of sages. Not only so, but the kind of analysis to which Mishnah- and Scripture-exegesis were subjected also applied to the exegesis of sage-stories.

That fact may be shown in three ways. First, just as Scripture supplied proof

---

[10]This argument, from redaction, runs parallel to the argument from rhetoric and logic to modes of thought, such as I offer in Parts One and Two of this book.

texts, so deeds or statements of sages provided proof texts. Second, just as a verse of Scripture or an explicit statement of the Mishnah resolved a disputed point, so what a sage said or did might be introduced into discourse as ample proof for settling a dispute. And third, it follows that just as Scripture or the Mishnah laid down Torah, so what a sage did or said laid down Torah. In the dimensions of the applied and practical reason by which the law unfolded, the sage found a comfortable place in precisely the taxonomic categories defined, to begin with, by both the Mishnah and Scripture. Let us examine a few substantial examples of the sorts of sustained discourse in biographical materials turned out by circles of sages. What we shall see is an important fact. Just as these circles composed units of discourse about the meaning of a Mishnah passage, a larger theoretical problem of law, the sense of scriptural verse, and the sayings and doings of scriptural heroes seen as sages, so they did the same for living sages themselves.

In the simplest example we see that two discrete sayings of a sage are joined together. The principle of conglomeration, therefore, is solely the name of the sage at hand. One saying has to do with overcoming the impulse to do evil, and the other has to do with the classifications of sages' program of learning. What the two subjects have in common is slight. But to the framer of the passage, that fact meant nothing. For he thought that compositions joined by the same tradent and authority — Levi and Simeon — should be made up.

B. Berakhot 4b.XXIII.

A. Said R. Levi bar Hama said R. Simeon b. Laqish, "A person should always provoke his impulse to do good against his impulse to do evil,

B. "as it is said, 'Provoke and do not sin' (Ps. 4:5).

C. "If [the good impulse] wins, well and good. If not, let him take up Torah study,

D. "as it is said, 'Commune with your own heart' (Ps. 4:5).

E. "If [the good impulse] wins, well and good. If not, let him recite the Shema,

F. "as it is said, 'upon your bed' (Ps. 4:5).

G. "If [the good impulse] wins, well and good. If not, let him remember the day of death,

H. "as it is said, 'And keep silent. Sela' (Ps. 4:5)."

I. And R. Levi bar Hama said R. Simeon b. Laqish said, "What is the meaning of the verse of Scripture, 'And I will give you the tables of stone, the law and the commandment, which I have written, that you may teach them' (Exod. 24:12).

J. "'The tables' [here] refers to the Ten Commandments.

K. "'Torah' refers to Scripture.

L. "'Commandment' refers to Mishnah.

M. "'Which I have written' refers to the Prophets and the Writings.

N. "'That you may teach them' refers to the Gemara.

O. "This teaches that all of them were given to Moses from Sinai."

The frame of the story at hand links A-H and I-O in a way unfamiliar to those accustomed to the principles of conglomeration in legal and biblical-exegetical compositions. In the former, a given problem or principle of law will tell us why one item is joined to some other. In the latter, a single verse of Scripture will account for the joining of two or more otherwise discrete units of thought. Here one passage, A-H, takes up Ps. 4:5; the other, I-O, Exod. 24:12. The point of the one statement hardly goes over the ground of the other. So the sole principle by which one item has joined the other is biographical: a record of what a sage said about topics that are, at best, contiguous, if related at all.

A second way of stringing together materials illustrative of the lives and teachings of sages is to join incidents involving a given authority or (as in the following case) two authorities believed to have stood in close relationship with one another, disciple and master, for instance. Often these stories go over the same ground in the same way. In the following, the two farewell stories make essentially the same point but in quite different language. What joins the stories is not only the shared theme but the fact that Eliezer is supposed to have studied with Yohanan b. Zakkai.

B. Sanhedrin 68A.II.

A. Our rabbis have taught on Tannaite authority:
B. When R. Eliezer fell ill, his disciples came in to pay a call on him. They said to him, "Our master, teach us the ways of life, so that through them we may merit the world to come."
C. He said to them, "Be attentive to the honor owing to your fellows, keep your children from excessive reflection, and set them among the knees of disciples of sages, and when you pray, know before whom you stand, and on that account you will merit the life of the world to come."
D. And when R. Yohanan b. Zakkai fell ill, his disciples came in to pay a call on him. When he saw them, he began to cry. His disciples said to him, "Light of Israel! Pillar at the right hand! Mighty hammer! On what account are you crying?"
E. He said to them, "If I were going to be brought before a mortal king, who is here today and tomorrow gone to the grave, who, should he be angry with me, will not be angry forever, and, if he should imprison me, will not imprison me forever, and if he should put me to death, whose sentence of death is not for eternity, and whom I can appease with the right words or bribe with money, even so, I should weep.
F. "But now that I am being brought before the King of kings of kings, the Holy One, blessed be he, who endures forever and ever, who, should he be angry with me, will be angry forever, and if he should imprison me, will imprison me forever, and if he should put me to death, whose sentence of death is for eternity, and whom I cannot appease with the right words or bribe with money,
G. "and not only so, but before me are two paths, one to the Garden of Eden and the other to Gehenna, and I do not know by which path I shall be brought,
H. "and should I not weep?"
I. They said to him, "Our master, bless us."
J. He said to them, "May it be God's will that the fear of Heaven be upon you as much as the fear of mortal man."

35

K. His disciples said, "Just so much?"

L. He said to them, "Would that it were that much. You should know that, when a person commits a transgression, he says, 'I hope no man sees me.'"

M. When he was dying, he said to them, "Clear out utensils from the house, because of the uncleanness [of the corpse, which I am about to impart when I die], and prepare a throne for Hezekiah king of Judah, who is coming."

The links between B-C and D-M are clear. First, we have stories about sages' farewells. Second, people took for granted, because of the lists of M. Abot 2:2ff., that Eliezer was disciple of Yohanan b. Zakkai. Otherwise, it is difficult to explain the joining of the stories, since they scarcely make the same point, go over the same matters, or even share a common literary or rhetorical form or preference. But a framer of a composition of lives of saints, who is writing a tractate on how saints die, will have found this passage a powerful one indeed.

Yet another approach to the utilization of tales about sages was to join together stories on a given theme but told about different sages. A tractate or a chapter of a tractate on a given theme, for example, suffering and its reward, can have emerged from the sort of collection that follows. The importance of the next item is that the same kinds of stories about different sages are strung together to make a single point.

B. Berakhot 5B.XXXI.

A. R. Hiyya bar Abba got sick. R. Yohanan came to him. He said to him, "Are these sufferings precious to you?"

B. He said to him, "I don't want them, I don't want their reward."

C. He said to him, "Give me your hand."

D. He gave him his hand, and [Yohanan] raised him up [out of his sickness].

E. R. Yohanan got sick. R. Hanina came to him. He said to him, "Are these sufferings precious to you?"

F. He said to him, "I don't want them. I don't want their reward."

G. He said to him, "Give me your hand."

H. He gave him his hand and [Hanina] raised him up [out of his sickness].

I. Why so? R. Yohanan should have raised himself up?

J. They say, "A prisoner cannot get himself out of jail."

B. Berakhot 5B.XXXII.

A. R. Eliezer got sick. R. Yohanan came to see him and found him lying in a dark room. [The dying man] uncovered his arm, and light fell [through the room]. [Yohanan] saw that R. Eliezer was weeping. He said to him, "Why are you crying? Is it because of the Torah that you did not learn sufficiently? We have learned: 'All the same are the ones who do much and do little, so long as each person will do it for the sake of heaven.'

B. "Is it because of insufficient income? Not everyone has the merit of seeing two tables [Torah and riches, as you have. You have been a master of Torah and also have enjoyed wealth].

36

C. "Is it because of children? Here is the bone of my tenth son [whom I buried, so it was no great loss not to have children, since you might have had to bury them]."

D. He said to him, "I am crying because of this beauty of mine which will be rotting in the ground."

E. He said to him, "For that it certainly is worth crying," and the two of them wept together.

F. He said to him, "Are these sufferings precious to you?"

G. He said to him, "I don't want them, I don't want their reward."

H. He said to him, "Give me your hand."

I. He gave him his hand, and [Yohanan] raised him up [out of his sickness].

B. Berakhot 5B.XXXIII.

A. Four hundred barrels of wine turned sour on R. Huna. R. Judah, brother of R. Sala the Pious, and rabbis came to see him (and some say it was R. Ada bar Ahba and rabbis). They said to him, "The master should take a good look at his deeds."

B. He said to them, "And am I suspect in your eyes?"

C. They said to him, "And is the Holy One, blessed be he, suspect of inflicting a penalty without justice?"

D. He said to them, "Has anybody heard anything bad about me? Let him say it."

E. They said to him, "This is what we have heard: the master does not give to his hired hand [the latter's share of] vine twigs [which are his right]."

F. He said to them, "Does he leave me any! He steals all of them to begin with."

G. They said to him, "This is in line with what people say: 'Go steal from a thief but taste theft too!' [Simon: If you steal from a thief, you also have a taste of it.]"

H. He said to them, "I pledge that I'll give them to him."

I. Some say that the vinegar turned back into wine, and some say that the price of vinegar went up so he sold it off at the price of wine.

The foregoing composite makes the same point several times: "Not them, not their reward." Sufferings are precious, but sages are prepared to forego the benefits. The formally climactic entry at XXXIII makes the point that, if bad things happen, the victim has deserved punishment. In joining these several stories about sages — two involving Yohanan, the third entirely separate — the compositor of the passage made his point by juxtaposing two like biographical snippets to a distinct one. Collections of stories about saints can have served quite naturally when formed into tractates on pious virtues, expressing these virtues through strong and pictorial language such as is before us.

The foregoing sources have shown two important facts. First, a principle of composition in the sages' circles was derived from interest in the teachings associated with a given sage, as well as in tales and stories told about a sage or groups of sages. The first of the passages shows us the simplest composition of sayings, the latter, an equivalent conglomeration of related stories. Up to this point, therefore, the reader will readily concede that biographical materials on sages, as much as Mishnah exegesis and Scripture exegesis, came forth out of circles of sages. But I have yet to show that such materials attained sufficient volume and cogency from large-scale compilations — conglomerates so substantial as to sustain entire books.

III. CHAPTERS AND TRACTATES ON LIVES OF SAGES: WHAT MIGHT HAVE BEEN

At the risk of taxing the reader's patience, I shall now demonstrate that, had the framers of large-scale rabbinic compositions wished, they could readily have made up tractates devoted to diverse sayings of a given authority (or, tradent-and-authority). What follows to demonstrate the possibility are two enormous compositions, which together can have made up as much as half of a Talmud chapter in volume. If anyone had wanted to compose a chapter around rabbinical authorities' names, he is thus shown to have had the opportunity.

The first shows us a string of sayings not only in a single set of names but also on discrete subjects. We also see how such a string of sayings could form the focus of exactly the kind of critical analysis and secondary amplification to which any other Talmudic passage would be subjected. So there can have been not only a Talmud based on the Mishnah and a midrash composition based on the Scripture but also a life of a saint (a gospel?) based on a set of rabbis' sayings. Here is the Talmud that can have served a collection of sayings of Yohanan-in-the-name-of-Simeon b. Yohai.

B. Berakhot 7B-8A.LIX.

A. [7B] Said R. Yohanan in the name of R. Simeon b. Yohai, "From the day on which the Holy One, blessed be he, created the world, there was no man who called the Holy One, blessed be he, 'Lord,' until Abraham came along and called him Lord.

B. "For it is said, 'And he said, O Lord, God, whereby shall I know that I shall inherit it' (Gen. 15:8)."

C. Said Rab, "Daniel too was answered only on account of Abraham.

D. "For it is said, 'Now therefore, O our God, hearken to the prayer of your servant and to his supplications and cause your face to shine upon your sanctuary that is desolate, for the Lord's sake' (Dan. 9:17).

E. "'For your sake' is what he should have said, but the sense is, 'For the sake of Abraham, who called you Lord.'"

B. Berakhot 7B-8A.LX.

A. And R. Yohanan said in the name of R. Simeon b. Yohai, "How do we know that people should not seek to appease someone when he is mad?

B. "As it is said, 'My face will go and then I will give you rest' (Exod. 33:14)."

38

B. Berakhot 7B-8A.LXI.

A. And R. Yohanan said in the name of R. Simeon b. Yohai, "From the day on which the Holy One, blessed be he, created his world, there was no one who praised the Holy One, blessed be he, until Leah came along and praised him.

B. "For it is said, 'This time I will praise the Lord' (Gen. 29:35)."

C. As to Reuben, said R. Eleazar, "Leah said, 'See what is the difference [the name of Reuben yielding reu (see) and ben (between)] between my son and the son of my father-in-law.

D. "The son of my father-in-law, even knowingly, sold off his birthright, for it is written, 'And he sold his birthright to Jacob' (Gen. 25:33).

E. "See what is written concerning him: 'And Esau hated Jacob' (Gen. 27:41), and it is written, 'And he said, is he not rightly named Jacob? for he has supplanted me these two times' (Gen. 27:36).

F. "My son, by contrast, even though Joseph forcibly took away his birthright, as it is written, 'But for as much as he defiled his father's couch, his birthright was given to the sons of Joseph' (1 Chron. 5:1), did not become jealous of him, for it is written, 'And Reuben heard it and delivered him out of their hand' (Gen. 37:21)."

G. As to the meaning of the name of Ruth, said R. Yohanan, "It was because she had the merit that David would come forth from her, who saturated (RWH) the Holy One, blessed be he, with songs and praises."

H. How do we know that a person's name affects [his life]?

I. Said R. Eleazar, "It is in line with the verse of Scripture: 'Come, behold the works of the Lord, who has made desolations in the earth' (Ps. 46:9).

J. "Do not read 'desolations' but 'names' [which the same root yields]."

B. Berakhot 7B-8A.LXII.

A. And R. Yohanan said in the name of R. Simeon b. Yohai, "Bringing a child up badly is worse in a person's house than the war of Gog and Magog.

B. "For it is said, 'A Psalm of David, when he fled from Absalom, his son' (Ps. 3:1), after which it is written, 'Lord how many are my adversaries become, many are they that rise up against me' (Ps. 3:2).

C. "By contrast, in regard to the war of Gog and Magog it is written, 'Why are the nations in an uproar? And why do the peoples mutter in vain?' (Ps. 2:1).

D. "But it is not written in that connection, 'How many are my adversaries become.'"

E. "A Psalm of David, when he fled from Absalom, his son (Ps. 3:1):

F. "'A Psalm of David'? It should be, 'A lamentation of David'!

G. Said R. Simeon b. Abishalom, "The matter may be compared to the case of a man against whom an outstanding bond was issued. Before he had paid it, he was sad. After he had paid it, he was glad.

H. "So too with David, when he the Holy One had said to him, 'Behold, I will raise up evil against you out of your own house,' (2 Sam. 2:11), he was sad.

I. "He thought to himself, 'Perhaps it will be a slave or a bastard child, who will not have pity on me.'

J. "When he saw that it was Absalom, he was happy. On that account, he said a psalm."

39

B. Berakhot 7B-8A.LXIII.

A. And R. Yohanan said in the name of R. Simeon b. Yohai, "It is permitted to contend with the wicked in this world,

B. "for it is said, 'Those who forsake the Torah praise the wicked, but those who keep the Torah contend with them' (Prov. 28:4)."

C. It has been taught on Tannaite authority along these same lines:

D. R. Dosetai bar Matun says, "It is permitted to contend with the wicked in this world, for it is said, 'Those who forsake the Torah praise the wicked, but those who keep the Torah contend with them' (Prov. 28:4)."

E. And if someone should whisper to you, "But is it not written, 'Do not contend with evildoers, nor be envious against those who work unrighteousness' (Ps. 37:1)," say to him, "Someone whose conscience bothers him thinks so.

F. "In fact, 'Do not contend with evildoers' means, do not be like them, 'nor be envious against those who work unrighteousness,' means, do not be like them.

G. "And so it is said, 'Let your heart not envy sinners, but fear the Lord all day' (Prov. 23:17)."

H. Is this the case? And lo, R. Isaac has said, "If you see a wicked person for whom the hour seems to shine, do not contend with him, for it is said, 'His ways prosper at all times' (Ps. 10:5).

I. "Not only so, but he wins in court, as it is said, 'Your judgments are far above, out of his sight' (Ps. 10:5).

J. "Not only so, but he overcomes his enemies, for it is said, 'As for all his enemies, he farts at them' (Ps. 10:5)."

K. There is no contradiction. The one [Isaac] addresses one's own private matters [in which case one should not contend with the wicked], but the other speaks of matters having to do with Heaven [in which case one should contend with them].

L. And if you wish, I shall propose that both parties speak of matters having to do with Heaven. There is, nonetheless, no contradiction. The one [Isaac] speaks of a wicked person on whom the hour shines, the other of a wicked person on whom the hour does not shine.

M. And if you wish, I shall propose that both parties speak of a wicked person on whom the hour shines, and there still is no contradiction.

N. The one [Yohanan, who says the righteous may contend with the wicked] speaks of a completely righteous person, the other [Isaac] speaks of someone who is not completely righteous.

O. For R. Huna said, "What is the meaning of this verse of Scripture: 'Why do you look, when they deal treacherously, and hold your peace, when the wicked swallows up the man that is more righteous than he' (Hab. 1:13)?

P. "Now can a wicked person swallow up a righteous one?

Q. "And lo, it is written, 'The Lord will not leave him in his hand' (Ps. 37:33). And it is further written, 'No mischief shall befall the righteous' (Prov. 12:21).

R. "The fact therefore is that he may swallow up someone who is more righteous than he, but he cannot swallow up a completely righteous man."

S. And if you wish, I shall propose that, when the hour shines for him, the situation is different.

B. Berakhot 7B-8A.LXIV.

A. And R. Yohanan said in the name of R. Simeon b. Yohai, "Beneath anyone who establishes a regular place for praying do that person's enemies fall.

B. "For it is said, 'And I will appoint a place for my people Israel, and I will plant them, that they may dwell in their own place and be disquieted no more, neither shall the children of wickedness afflict them any more as at the first' (2 Sam. 7:10)."

C. R. Huna pointed to a contradiction between two verses of Scripture: "It is written, 'To afflict them,' and elsewhere, 'To exterminate them' (1 Chron. 17:9).

D. "To begin with, merely to afflict them, but, at the end, to exterminate them."

B. Berakhot 7B-8A.LXV.

A. And R. Yohanan said in the name of R. Simeon b. Yohai, "Greater is personal service to Torah than learning in Torah [so doing favors for a sage is of greater value than studying with him].

B. "For it is said, 'Here is Elisha, the son of Shaphat, who poured water on the hands of Elijah' (2 Kings 3:11).

C. "It is not said, 'who learned' but 'who poured water.'

D. "This teaches that greater is service to Torah than learning in Torah."

It is not difficult to pick up the main beams of the foregoing construction, since they are signified by Yohanan-Simeon sayings, LIX.A, LX.A, LXI.A, LXII.A, LXIII.A, LXIV.A, LXV.A — seven entries in line. The common theme is not prayer; no other topic is treated in a cogent way either. The sort of inner coherence to which any student of the Bavli is accustomed does not pass before us. Rather we have a collection of wise thoughts on diverse topics, more in the manner of Proverbs than in the style of the great intellects behind the sustained reasoning in passages of the Bavli and much of the Yerushalmi as well. What is interesting is that, at a later stage, other pertinent materials have been inserted, for example, Rab's at LIX.C-E, and so on down. There is no reason to imagine that these sayings were made up in response to Yohanan-Simeon's statement. Quite to the contrary, framed in their own terms, the sayings were presumably tacked on at a point at which the large-scale construction of Yohanan-Simeon was worked over for a purpose beyond the one intended by the original compositor. For what he wanted to do he did, which is, compose a collection of Yohanan-Simeon sayings. If he hoped that his original collection would form part of a larger composition on Yohanan, he surely was disappointed. But even if he imagined that he would make up material for compositions of lives and sayings of saints, he cannot have expected his little collection to end up where and how it did, as part of a quite different corpus of writing from one in which a given authority had his say or in which stories were told in some sort of sensible sequence about a particular sage. The type of large-scale composition, for which our imagined compositor did his work, in the end never came into being in the rabbinic canon.

41

In the following, still longer example I begin with the passage to which the entire composition, organized in the name of a tradent and a sage, is attached. At B. Berakhot 6B/1:1 XLI, we have a statement that a synagogue should have a regular quorum. Then the next passage, 1:1 XLII, makes the secondary point that a person should pray in a regular place — a reasonable amplification of the foregoing. That is, just as there should be a quorum routinely organized in a given location, so should an individual routinely attach himself to a given quorum. This statement is given by Helbo in Huna's name. What follows is a sizable set of sayings by Helbo in Huna's name, all of them on the general theme of prayer but none of them on the specific point at hand. Still more interesting, just as in the foregoing, the passage as a whole was composed so that the Helbo-Huna materials themselves are expanded and enriched with secondary accretions. For instance, at XLIII the base materials are given glosses of a variety of types. All in all, we see what we may call a little tractate in the making. But, as we shall hardly have to repeat, no one in the end created a genre of rabbinic literature to accommodate the vast collections of available compositions on sages' sayings and doings.

B. Berakhot 6B.XLI.

    A.   Said R. Yohanan, "When the Holy One, blessed be he, comes to a synagogue and does not find ten present, he forthwith becomes angry.

    B.   "For it is said, 'Why when I came was there no one there? When I called, there was no answer' (Isa. 50:2)."

B. Berakhot 6B.XLII.

    A.   Said R. Helbo said R. Huna, "For whoever arranges a regular place for praying, the God of Abraham is a help, and when he dies, they say for him, 'Woe for the humble man, woe for the pious man, one of the disciples of Abraham, our father.'

    B.   "And how do we know in the case of Abraham, our father, that he arranged a regular place for praying?

    C.   "For it is written, 'And Abraham got up early in the morning on the place where he had stood' (Gen. 19:27).

    D.   "'Standing' refers only to praying, for it is said, 'Then Phinehas stood up and prayed' (Ps. 106:30)."

    E.   Said R. Helbo to R. Huna, "He who leaves the synagogue should not take large steps."

    F.   Said Abayye, "That statement applies only when one leaves, but when he enters, it is a religious duty to run [to the synagogue].

    G.   "For it is said, 'Let us run to know the Lord' (Hos. 6:3)."

    H.   Said R. Zira, "When in the beginning I saw rabbis running to the lesson on the Sabbath, I thought that the rabbis were profaning the Sabbath. But now that I have heard what R. Tanhum said R. Joshua b. Levi said,

    I.   "namely, 'A person should always run to take up a matter of law, and even on the Sabbath, as it is said, "They shall walk after the Lord who shall roar like a lion [for he shall roar, and the children shall come hurrying]" (Hos. 11:10),'

    J.   "I too run."

B. Berakhot 6B.XLIII.

A. Said R. Zira, "The reward for attending the lesson is on account of running [to hear the lesson, not necessarily on account of what one has learned.]"

B. Said Abayye, "The reward for attending the periodic public assembly [of rabbis] is on account of the crowding together."

C. Said Raba [to the contrary], "The reward for repeating what one has heard is in reasoning about it."

D. Said R. Papa, "The reward for attending a house of mourning is on account of one's preserving silence there."

E. Said Mar Zutra, "The reward for observing a fast day lies in the acts of charity one performs on that day."

F. Said R. Sheshet, "The reward for delivering a eulogy lies in raising the voice."

G. Said R. Ashi, "The reward for attending a wedding lies in the words [of compliment paid to the bride and groom]."

B. Berakhot 6B.XLIV.

A. Said R. Huna, "Whoever prays behind the synagogue is called wicked,

B. "as it is said, 'The wicked walk round about' (Ps. 12:9)."

C. Said Abayye, "That statement applies only in the case of one who does not turn his face toward the synagogue, but if he turns his face toward the synagogue, we have no objection."

D. There was a certain man who would say his prayers behind the synagogue and did not turn his face toward the synagogue. Elijah came by and saw him. He appeared to him in the guise of a Tai Arab.

E. He said to him, "Are you now standing with your back toward your master?" He drew his sword and killed him.

F. One of the rabbis asked R. Bibi bar Abayye, and some say, R. Bibi asked R. Nahman bar Isaac, "What is the meaning of the verse, 'When vileness is exalted among the sons of men' (Ps. 12:9)?"

G. He said to him, "This refers to matters that are exalted, which people treat with contempt."

H. R. Yohanan and R. Eleazar both say, "When a person falls into need of the help of other people, his face changes color like the kerum, for it is said, 'As the kerum is to be reviled among the sons of men' (Ps. 12:9)."

I. What is the meaning of kerum?

J. When R. Dimi came, he said, "There is a certain bird among the coast towns, called the kerum. When the sun shines, it turns many colors."

K. R. Ammi and R. Assi both say, "[When a person turns to others for support], it is as if he is judged to suffer the penalties of both fire and water.

L. "For it is said, 'When you caused men to ride over our heads, we went through fire and through water' (Ps. 66:12)."

B. Berakhot 6B.XLV.

A. And R. Helbo said R. Huna said, "A person should always be attentive at the afternoon prayer.

43

B. "For lo, Elijah was answered only at the afternoon prayer.
C. "For it is said, 'And it came to pass at the time of the offering of the late afternoon offering, that Elijah the prophet came near and said, "Hear me, O Lord, hear me'" (1 Kings 18:36-37)."
D. "Hear me" so fire will come down from heaven.
E. "Hear me" that people not say it is merely witchcraft.
F. R. Yohanan said, "[A person should also be attentive about] the evening prayer.
G. "For it is said, 'Let my prayer be set forth as incense before you, the lifting up of my hands as the evening sacrifice' (Ps. 141:2)."
H. R. Nahman bar Isaac said, "[A person should also be attentive about] the morning prayer.
I. "For it is said, 'O Lord, in the morning you shall hear my voice, in the morning I shall order my prayer to you, and will look forward' (Ps. 5:4)."

B. Berakhot 6B.XLVI.

A. And R. Helbo said R. Huna said, "Whoever enjoys a marriage banquet and does not felicitate the bridal couple violates five 'voices.'
B. "For it is said, 'The voice of joy and the voice of gladness, the voice of the bridegroom and the voice of the bride, the voice of those who say, "Give thanks to the Lord of hosts'" (Jer. 33:11)."
C. And if he does felicitate the couple, what reward does he get?
D. Said R. Joshua b. Levi, "He acquires the merit of the Torah, which was handed down with five voices.
E. "For it is said, 'And it came to pass on the third day, when it was morning, that there were voices [thus two], and lightnings, and a thick cloud upon the mount, and the voice of a horn, and when the voice of the horn waxed louder, 'Moses spoke and God answered him by a voice.' (Exod. 19:16, 19) [thus five voices in all]."
F. Is it so [that there were only five voices]?
G. And lo, it is written, "And all the people saw the voices" (Exod. 20:15). [So this would make seven voices.]
H. These voices came before the giving of the Torah [and do not count].
I. R. Abbahu said, "It is as if the one [who felicitated the bridal couple] offered a thanksgiving offering.
J. "For it is said, 'Even of them that bring thanksgiving offerings into the house of the Lord' (Jer. 33:11)."
K. R. Nahman bar Isaac said, "It is as if he rebuilt one of the ruins of Jerusalem.
L. "For it is said, 'For I will cause the captivity of the land to return as at the first, says the Lord' (Jer. 33:11)."

B. Berakhot 6B.XLVII.

A. And R. Helbo said R. Huna said, "The words of any person in whom is fear of Heaven are heard.
B. "For it is said, 'The end of the matter, all having been heard: fear God and keep his commandments, for this is the whole man' (Qoh. 12:13)."
C. What is the meaning of the phrase, "For this is the whole man" (Qoh. 12:13)?
D. Said R. Eleazar, "Said the Holy One, blessed be he, 'The entire world has been

44

created only on account of this one.'"

E.   R. Abba bar Kahana said, "This one is worth the whole world."

F.   Simeon b. Zoma says, "The entire world was created only to accompany this
     one."

B. Berakhot 6B.XLVIII.

A.   And R. Helbo said R. Huna said, "Whoever knows that his fellow regularly
     greets him should greet the other first.

B.   "For it is said, 'Seek peace and pursue it' (Ps. 34:15).

C.   "If he greeted him and the other did not reply, the latter is called a thief.

D.   "For it is said, 'It is you who have eaten up the vineyard, the spoil of the poor
     is in your houses' (Isa. 3:14)."

What we noted in connection with the Yohanan-Simeon collection needs no
restatement here. The scope and dimensions of the passage prove impressive.
Again we must wonder for what sort of composition the framer of the Helbo-Huna
collection planned his writing. Whatever it was, it hardly fit the ultimate destination
of his work.

IV. THE STANDING AND AUTHORITY OF THE SAGE

One reason for not forming gospels can have been that the sage did not stand
at the leveln of the Torah, while the Mishnah and Scripture constituted the Torah.
Hence forming documents around the lives of the sage, as much as around the
amplification of Scripture and the Mishnah, can have made no sense. But the
opposite is the fact. The sage stood at that same level of authority as did the Torah,
on the one side, and the Mishnah, on the other. Therefore the failure to compose
gospels alongside Midrash-compilations and Mishnah-exegesis is not to be explained away as an byproduct of the conception of revelation through words but not
through persons that is imputed to the Judaism of the dual Torah. Quite to the
contrary, God reveals the Torah not only through words handed down from Sinai
in the form of the Torah, written and oral, but also through the lives and deeds of
saints, that is, sages. Reference to the discussion of Korah in Chapter Two will
suffice to make the simple point that the same modes of exegetical inquiry
pertaining to the Mishnah and Scripture apply without variation to statements made
by rabbis of the contemporary period themselves.

We turn to the way in which the rabbis of the Yerushalmi proposed to resolve
differences of opinion. Precisely in the same way in which talmudic rabbis settled
disputes in the Mishnah and so attained a consensus about the law of the Mishnah,
they handled disputes among themselves. The importance of that fact for our
argument again is simple. The rabbis, represented in the Yerushalmi, treated their
own contemporaries exactly as they treated the then-ancient authorities of the
Mishnah. In their minds the status accorded to the Mishnah, as a derivative of the
Torah, applied equally to sages' teachings. In the following instance we see how

the same discourse attached to (1) a Mishnah rule is assigned as well to one in (2) the Tosefta and, at the end, to differences among (3) the Yerushalmi's authorities.

Yerushalmi Ketubot 5:1.VI.

A. R. Jacob bar Aha, R. Alexa in the name of Hezekiah: "The law accords with the view of R. Eleazar b. Azariah, who stated, If she was widowed or divorced at the stage of betrothal, the virgin collects only two hundred zuz and the widow, a maneh. If she was widowed or divorced at the stage of a consummated marriage, she collects the full amount [M. Ket. 5:1E,D]."

B. R. Hananiah said, "The law accords with the view of R. Eleazar b. Azariah."

C. Said Abayye, "They said to R. Hananiah, 'Go and shout [outside whatever opinion you like.' But] R. Jonah, R. Zeira in the name of R. Jonathan said, 'The law accords with the view of R. Eleazar b. Azariah.' [Yet] R. Yosa bar Zeira in the name of R. Jonathan said, 'The law does not accord with the view of R. Eleazar b. Azariah.' [So we do not in fact know the decision.]"

D. Said R. Yose, "We had a mnemonic: Hezekiah and R. Jonathan both say one thing."

E. For it has been taught:

F. He whose son went abroad, and whom they told, "Your son has died,"

G. and who went and wrote over all his property to someone else as a gift,

H. and whom they afterward informed that his son was yet alive —

I. his deed of gift remains valid.

J. R. Simeon b. Menassia says, "His deed of gift is not valid, for if he had known that his son was alive, he would never have made such a gift" [T. Ket. 4:14E-H].K. Now R. Jacob bar Aha [=A] said, "The law is in accord with the view of R. Eleazar b. Azariah, and the opinion of R. Eleazar b. Azariah is the same in essence as that of R. Simeon b. Menassia."

L. Now R. Yannai said to R. Hananiah, "Go and shout [outside whatever you want].

M. "But, said R. Yose bar Zeira in the name of R. Jonathan, 'The law is not in accord with R. Eleazar b. Azariah.'"

N. But in fact the case was to be decided in accord with the view of R. Eleazar b. Azariah.

What is important here is that the Talmud makes no distinction whatever when deciding the law of disputes (1) in the Mishnah, (2) in the Tosefta, and (3) among talmudic rabbis. The same already-formed colloquy applied at the outset to the Mishnah's dispute is then held equally applicable to the Tosefta's. The process of thought is the main thing, without regard to the document to which the process applies. Scripture, the Mishnah, the sage — the three spoke with equal authority. True, one had to come into alignment with the other, the Mishnah with Scripture, the sage with the Mishnah. But it was not the case that one component of the Torah, of God's word to Israel, stood within the sacred circle, another beyond. Interpretation and what was interpreted, exegesis and text, belonged together. The sage, or rabbi, constitutes the third component in a tripartite canon of the Torah, because, while Scripture and the Mishnah govern what the sage knows, in the Yerushalmi as in the Bavli it is the sage who authoritatively speaks about them. What sages were willing to do to the Mishnah in the Yerushalmi and Bavli is precisely what they were prepared to do to Scripture — impose upon it their own judgment of its meaning.

V. THE SAGE AND THE TORAH

The sage speaks with authority about the Mishnah and the Scripture. As much as they, he therefore has authority deriving from revelation. He himself may participate in the process of revelation. There is no material difference. Since that is so, the sage's book, whether the Yerushalmi or the Bavli to the Mishnah or Midrash to Scripture, is Torah, that is, revealed by God. It also forms part of the Torah, a fully canonical document. The reason, then, is that the sage is like Moses, "our rabbi," who received torah and wrote the Torah. So while the canon was in three parts — Scripture, Mishnah, sage — the sage, in saying what the other parts meant and in embodying that meaning in his life and thought, took primacy of place. If no document organized itself around sayings and stories of sages, it was because that was superfluous. Why so? Because all documents, equally, whether Scripture, whether Mishnah, whether Yerushalmi, gave full and complete expression of deeds and deliberations of sages, beginning, after all, with Moses, our rabbi.

CHAPTER FOUR
FROM GOSPEL TO AUTHORSHIP:
THE REASON WHY

I.   SAGE-STORIES, NO GOSPELS ABOUT SAGES

The sage falls into the classification of the Torah. That seems a solid reason not only for making up stories about sages but also for composing those stories into large-scale documents, such as tractates (for the Mishnah) or Midrash-compilations (for Scripture). Accordingly, the fact just now demonstrated in Chapter Four brings us to ask how sage-stories compare with Scripture-stories, that is to say, stories in the rabbinic canon that amplify or otherwise augment scriptural themes or provide exegesis of verses of Scripture. Only if we differentiate the sage-story from the Scripture-story shall we grasp the full difference effected in the redactional process by those who determined to collect into large-scale compositions one sort of story but not the other. And that fact is critical to our consideration of why there are no gospels in the canon of the Judaism of the dual Torah. When we recognize that sage-stories do differ from Scripture-stories, we shall begin to move ahead in the larger problem of differentiation at hand. For the present purpose we turn in particular to The Fathers According to Rabbi Nathan. Let me explain why.

The one document identified thus far to serve as a medium for gospels is The Fathers According to Rabbi Nathan, an amplification of The Fathers (Avot), to which we now turn for an example of the canonical alternative to a gospel. The reason is that that document's authorship made a decision to make use of a kind of writing found of no interest by the authorship of the document subject to amplification. The authorship of The Fathers According to Rabbi Nathan clearly found inadequate the mode of intelligible discourse and the medium of expression selected by the framers of the document they chose to extend. The authorship of The Fathers used no stories and neglected narrative as a medium of discourse. The later writers by contrast resorted to a mode of intelligible discourse, narrative, omitted by the earlier one[11]. Not only so, but among the narratives utilized in their composition, they selected one, the story about a sage, or, as I shall call it, the sage-story, for closest attention and narrative development[12].

II.   SAGE-STORIES AND SCRIPTURE-STORIES: THE DIFFERENCES

I start by demonstrating that the sage-story is fundamentally to be distinguished from the Scripture-story. To do so, I simply set side-by-side stories about a

---

[11] I do not treat as narrative the use of "One day he saw and said...," which serves as a setting for a saying. In such a usage I find no story-line, no point of tension, no resolution of tension, no beginning, middle, end, merely a set-piece stage-setting. That does not seem to me to present an exception to the rule stated here.

[12] In my *Judaism and Story, The Evidence of The Fathers According to Rabbi Nathan* (Chicago, 1988: University of Chicago Press) I provide a taxonomy of narratives of that document. Sage-story is the one that interests us here.

scriptural hero and a sage, as the authorship of The Fathers According to Rabbi Nathan presents both sorts of stories. The difference is not merely that one speaks of a hero that appears in Scripture, the other of one that derives from the chain of tradition of the Oral Torah. Much to the contrary! The contrast will show us right at the outset that quite different narrative conventions apply to the two distinct topics, the hero of Scripture, the hero of sagacity. Stories about the archetypal sage, Moses, "our lord" turn out not very different from stories on other scriptural topics.

The striking contrast in the narrative qualities of the story about Hanina's and Abraham's beasts, given in what follows, tells the whole tale. Our example deals with a hero of the written Torah, Abraham, and one of the oral Torah, Hanina b. Dosa. The same point is made with reference to both figures. So the important point of difference will occur solely in the distinctive modes of telling the two stories. The narrative conventions do differ substantially:

The Fathers According to Rabbi Nathan VIII:VI.1

    A.   Just as the righteous men in ancient times were pious, so their cattle were pious.

    B.   They say that the cattle of Abraham, our father, never went into a house which contained an idol,

    C.   as it is said, *For I have cleared the house and made room for the camels* (Gen. 24:31), meaning, *I have cleared the house of teraphim.*

    D.   And on what account does Scripture say, And made room *for the camels?*

    E.   This teaches that they would not enter Laban the Aramaean's house until they had cleared away all the idols from before them.

VIII:VI.2

    A.   There was the case of the ass of R. Hanina b. Dosa, which bandits stole and tied up in the courtyard. They set before it straw, barley and water, but it would not eat or drink.

    B.   They said, "Why should we leave it here to die and make a stink for us in teh courtyard? They went and opened the gate and sent it out, and it went along, braying util it came to the house of R. Hanina B. Dosa.

    C.   When it got near the house, [Hanina's] son heard its braying.

    D.   He said to him, "Father, it appears to me that the braying is like the braying of our beast."

    E.   He said to him, "My son, open the gate for it, for it must be nearly dying of starvation."

    F.   He went and opened the gate for it, and put before it straw, barley and water, and it ate and drank.

    G.   Therefore they say: Just as the righteous men in ancient times were pious, so their cattle were pious.

The contrast between the narrative traits of the two stories could not be drawn more sharply. In the story about the biblical hero, we have proof-text after proof-text. In fact we have nothing like a narrative. "They say" that such and such did or did not do so and so hardly tells an engaging story. Then comes a lesson, E. By contrast, making the same point, the case involving Hanina's ass does involve a fully expounded narrative. The hero is the animal, not the authority. The story works out its message without the need for G, since the point is made within the limits and discipline of the story itself, with its point of tension — the stolen beast that finds its way home, that is released because of its own pious behavior — and the resolution thereof. The juxtaposed stories indicate that, where the written Torah supplies the materials for a narrative, the consequent tale hardly qualifies as a story at all.

This brings us back to those questions that define our reading of stories on sages. First, we wish to find out whether the subject-matter — sages' lives and deeds — imposes narrative literary conventions that differ from those that guide writers of stories about Scriptural figures. On the surface we come across numerous obvious differences in narrative convention. Three seem to me definitive:

[1] the story about a sage has a beginning, middle, and end, and the story about a sage also rests not only on verbal exchanges ("he said to him..., he said to him..."), but on (described) action.

[2] the story about a sage unfolds from a point of tension and conflict to a clear resolution and remission of the conflict.

[3] the story about a sage rarely invokes a verse of Scripture and never serves to prove a proposition concerning the meaning of a verse of Scripture.

What about Scripture-stories? The traits of stories about scriptural figures and themes in retrospect prove opposite:

[1] in the story about a scriptural hero there is no beginning, middle, and end, and little action. The burden of the narrative is carried by "he said to him..., he said to him...." Described action is rare and plays slight role in the unfolding of the narrative. Often the narrative consists of little more than a setting for a saying, and the point of the narrative is conveyed not through what is told but through the cited saying.

[2] the story about a scriptural hero is worked out as a tableau, with description of the components of the stationary tableau placed at the center. There is little movement, no point of tension that is resolved.

[3] the story about a scriptural hero always invokes verses from Scripture and makes the imputation of meaning to those verses the center of interest.

The fact relevant to our question is that, while theologically the sage enjoys a place in the Torah, in literary terms the sage is clearly differentiated from a scriptural

51

figure. Presented with stories taken from our document that lack all markings to indicate their subject-matter, we could readily identify those focused upon scriptural heroes as distinct from those centered upon sages. When the narrators wish to talk about sages, they invoked one set of narrative conventions, deemed appropriate to that topic, and when they turned to make up stories on scriptural heroes and topics, they appealed to quite different narrative conventions.

III. THE TOPICAL REPERTOIRE OF SAGE-STORIES: THE INSUFFICIENCY OF SAGE-STORIES FOR FORMING GOSPELS

The sage-stories in The Fathers According to Rabbi Nathan do not cover a broad variety of topics but attend only to a few, selected subjects. Only certain aspects of the lives and doings of sages demanded attention, and then for highly particular purposes. That fact again has important bearing upon our problem. What it tells us is that while the raw-materials for gospels — miracle-stories, biographical materials — do present themselves, sage-stories in point of fact cannot in the end coalesce into gospels. They serve a different purpose from biography, and biography in the end does not define the classification for these stories. I shall show that fact in some detail, because it carries us a considerable distance toward our goal.

To demonstrate that fact, I classify the stories in The Fathers According to Rabbi Nathan by topics, because the most superficial trait, subject-matter. The sage-stories in this document[13] attend to only four topics: the sage's beginning in Torah-study, his character and his deeds in relationship to the Torah, the role of the sage in important historical events, and at the end, the death of sages. Out of such a repertoire, a gospel is not possible. In point of fact, the sole theme characteristic of sage-stories in The Fathers According to Rabbi Nathan is the theme of the Torah, study of the Torah and the power gained by study of the Torah. Let me state with emphasis the main point at hand:

Sage-stories turn out not to tell about sages at all; they are stories about the Torah personified.

Sage-stories cannot yield a gospel because they are not about sages anyhow. They are about the Torah. Gospels by contrast tell the life of a human being, whom the narrator represents as holy and capable of miracles. The sage-stories do not differentiate one sage from another and do not underline traits of individuality. Quite to the contrary, the sage is represented always as exemplary, rarely as individual and distinct from other sages except by the standard of the Torah: more

---

[13]We could, of course, collect among diverse conanical writings of the formative period stories on all the subjects not treated in a coherent setting in the document under study. That underlines two points critical to my argument. First, the materials for gospels were at hand. Second, when sage-stories formed the definite component of a document, it was not so as to produce anything like gospels.

or less Torah, not difference between one sage's Torah and another sage's Torah. The sage-story, dealing with the individual, homogenizes sage with sage. The gospel does just the opposite, with its focus on the uniqueness of the hero[14].

A list of the topics of sage-stories in The Fathers According to Rabbi Nathan that in fact are neglected, for example, the sage's childhood and wonderful precociousness in Torah-study, the sage's supernatural deeds, the sage's everyday administration of the community's affairs, the sage's life with other sages and with disciples — such a list could be extended over many pages. But it suffices to notice that our document has chosen a highly restricted list of topics, but then differentiated, within these topics, by telling quite diverse stories about different sages as to their origins, deaths, and the like. The upshot is that when the authorship of The Fathers According to Rabbi Nathan resorted to narrative in general and story-telling in particular, with special attention to sage-stories, those compositors had in mind a very particular purpose and message indeed. There was nothing random or episodic in their choices of topics, and the medium of story-telling served the message conveyed by the story set forth in our composition.

IV. THE BIRTH OF JESUS CHRIST IN MATTHEW'S GOSPEL AND THE ORIGINS OF AQIBA AND ELIEZER

The contrast between sage-story and Gospel-story is readily drawn when we compare Matthew's story of the birth of Jesus Christ with the stories about the origins of Aqiba and Eliezer in The Fathers According to Rabbi Nathan. The interest of the former is well-known. "Now the birth of Jesus Christ took place in this way" (Mt. 2:18): the birth of the child was announced to the virgin-mother, Mary. Herod was told that the king of the Jews has been born. The Magi worshipped the infant. Herod killed the newborn babes; Joseph and Mary fled to Egypt. When Herod died, Joseph and Mary returned. And so on. The well-known story covers a variety of details. Not a single detail concerning the annunciation of the birth, the conditions of the birth, or the immediate events that succeeded the birth, of a sage, exists in the entire rabbinic canon of late antiquity. But the specific contrast I wish to draw concerns not what people do not say, but the things they choose to emphasize. We have in our document no birth-stories at all, but we do have "origins-in-Torah" stories, to which we turn.

The Fathers According to Rabbi Nathan contains stories of not the birth but "the origins" as masters of the Torah of two sages, Aqiba and Eliezer. By "origins," the story-tellers mean the beginnings of the Torah-study of a famed authority. Life begins at birth, but when we wish to tell sage-stories, beginnings are measured

---

[14]The fact that hagiography tends toward a certain homogeneity is not pertinent here. A study of hagiographical literature will yield differentiation between one saint and another, so that while all saints in common exhibit certain virtues, nonetheless, each sait bears traits of his or her own, which make the stories individual, even though of a common type.

differently. The sage begins life when he begins Torah-study. And the sages whose origins are found noteworthy both began in mature years, not in childhood (despite the repeated emphasis of The Fathers upon the unique value of beginning Torah-study in childhood). The proposition implicit in origins-stories then is that any male may start his Torah-study at any point in life and hope for true distinction in the Torah-community. But that does not account for the germ of the story, the critical tension that creates an event worthy of narrative, that poses a question demanding an answer, a problem requiring a solution through a tale with a beginning, middle, and end.

As everyone knows, Matthew tells the origins of a supernatural person, a unique individual. The critical tension of "origins" derives from the formation of supernatural, in contrast to natural, *relationships*. Life begins at the womb. But Torah-life does not begin in the natural birth, treated as supernatural in one case only, but begins at a supernatural birth of an already-existing natural man, and, within that logic, there must be a tension between the natural beginning and the supernatural one. It is expressed through contrasting natural ties and relationships, to father and mother and brothers and sisters, or to one's wife, and supernatural ties to Torah-study. When a man undertakes to study the Torah, in the stories before us he abandons his natural relationships to his family, in the one case to his wife, in the other to his father. The point of origination of the sage marks the beginning of the wedding of the sage to the Torah, with the concommitant diminution of his relationship to his wife, who may be abandoned and indeed required to support the nascent sage's children as well as herself. The nascent sage furthermore gains a new father, the master or sage, and cuts his ties to the natural father, with the consequence that he loses his share in the estate to be provided by the father. These tensions generate the stories before us.

While told each in its own terms and subject to differentiation from the other, the stories make essentially the same point, which is that one can begin Torah-study in mature years and progress to the top, when one does so, one also goes from poverty to wealth through public recognition of one's mastery of the Torah, and a range of parallel propositions along the same lines. The supernatural relationship, which has superceded the natural ones to wife and father, generates glory and honor, riches and fame, for the sage, and, through reflection, for the natural family as well. That is the point of the stories of the origins of sages, which take up what is clearly a pressing question and answer it in a powerful way. (I give in bold-face type citations of language in The Fathers.)

The Fathers According to Rabbi Nathan VI:IV.1

A. Another comment on the statement, **And wallow in the dust of their feet:**

B. This refers to R. Eliezer.

C. **...and drink in their words with gusto:**

D. This refers to R. Aqiba.

This pericope serves as a prologue to the vast stories to follow. first on Aqiba, then on Eliezer.

VI:V.1

A. How did R. Aqiba begin [his Torah-study]?

B. They say: He was forty years old and had never repeated a tradition. One time he was standing at the mouth of a well. He thought to himself, "Who carved out this stone?"

C. They told him, "It is the water that is perpetually falling on it every day."

D. They said to him, "Aqiba, do you not read Scripture? *The water wears away stones* (Job. 4:19)?"

E. On the spot R. Aqiba constructed in his own regard an argument a *fortiori:* now if something soft can [Goldin:] wear down something hard, words of Torah, which are as hard as iron, how much the more so should wear down my heart, which is made of flesh and blood."

F. On the spot he repented [and undertook] to study the Torah.

G. He and his son went into study session before a childrens' teacher, saying to him, "My lord, teach me Torah."

H. R. Aqiba took hold of one end of the tablet, and his son took hold of the other end. The teacher wrote out for him *Alef Bet* and he learned it, *Alef Tav* and he learned it, the *Torah of the Priests* [the books of Leviticus and Numbers] and he learned it. He went on learning until he had learned the entire Torah.

I. He went and entered study-sessions before R. Eliezer and before R. Joshua. He said to them, "My lords, open up for me the reasoning of the Mishnah."

J. When they had stated one passage of law, he went and sat by himself and said, "Why is this *alef* written? why is this *bet* written? Why is this statement made?" He went and asked them and, in point of fact, [Goldin:] reduced them to silence.

Clearly, our opening component in the *magnalia Aqibae* is a narrative. The tone and program establish the mood of narrative: he was...he had...he did.... But how shall we classify the narrative, and by what criteria? One important criterion is whether the narrative describes a situation or tells about something that happened, with a beginning, middle, and end. The one is at rest, the other in movement. These constitute questions with objective answers. Do we have a tableau or a story, or, for that matter, a parable, or any of those other types of narratives we have already classified? By the simple criterion that a story has a beginning, middle, end, which dictate points of narrative tension, and a clearly delineated program of action, we have a story. The components do more than merely set up pieces in a static tableau. They flow from one to the next and yield movement — hence narrative action.

What about the Scripture-story? The blatant differences require slight amplification. We note that verses of Scripture scarcely intervene, and there is no focus on the exegesis of a verse of Scripture. At D, Aqiba and his interlocutors do not interpret the verse but simply draw upon its statement of fact. A sage-story, as I said,

55

following the pattern determined by Aristotle has a beginning, middle, and end: movement from tension to resolution. In the present story there is a beginning: he had not studied; a middle, he went and studied; and an end, following Goldin's persuasive rendering, "he reduced them to silence." True, the action takes place mainly in what Aqiba thought, rather than in what he did. But in the nature of things, the action of going to study the Torah forms the one genuinely dramatic deed that is possible with the present subject-matter. The beginning then works its way out at B-F. The middle is at G-H: Aqiba was so humble as to study with his own son. Then at I-J we have a climax and conclusion: Aqiba proved so profound in his question-asking that he reduced the great authorities to silence. That conclusion hardly flows from A-H, but it is absolutely necessary to make the entire sequence into a cogent story. Otherwise we have merely bits and pieces of an uncompleted narrative.

Let us proceed to what follows in the context of the telling of the story of Aqiba's origins. Here we shall see most strikingly how, given the opportunity for a sustained narrative of the life of a man, the framers of The Fathers According to Rabbi Nathan do not exploit the occasion. Rather than dealing with other tales about the man, they focus upon the theme which he has served to realize in his own life, Torah-study.

VI:V.2

A. R. Simeon b. Eleazar says, "I shall make a parable for you. To what is the matter comparable? To a stonecutter who was cutting stone in a quarry. One time he took his chisel and went and sat down on the mountain and started to chip away little sherds from it. People came by and said to him, 'What are you doing?'

B. "He said to them, 'Lo, I am going to uproot the mountain and move it into the Jordan River."

C. "They said to him, 'You will never be able to uproot the entire mountain.'

D. "He continued chipping away at the mountain until he came to a huge boulder. He quarried underneath it and unearthed it and uprooted it and tossed it into the Jordan.'

E. "He said to the boulder, 'This is not your place, but that is your place.'

F. "Likewise this is what R. Aqiba did to R. Eliezer and to R. Joshua."

The parable without F simply says that with patience one may move mountains. The parable by itself — not applied — amplifies or at least continues VI:V.1.E, the power of words of Torah to wear down the hard heart of a human being. But the parable proves particular to the preceding story, since the add-on, E, F, applies the parable to VI:V.1.J, the humiliation of Joshua and Eliezer. We may wonder whether, without the announcement at A that we have a parable, the parabolic character of the tale would have impressed us. The answer is that the general traits of a parable — an anonymous illustration in concrete and everyday terms of an abstract proposition — do occur in A-D, at which point the par worked out its proposition: "he continued chipping away...." Even E, without F, can remain within

56

the limits of the announced proposition of the parable, that is, the power of patience and persistence. So only F is jarring. It clearly serves the redactor's purpose. It does not transform the parable into a story (!), since it does not impose upon the prior narrative that particularity and concrete one-time-ness that form the indicative traits of the story alone. In all, we may dismiss from the evidence of the story the present complement to the foregoing.

VI: V.3

    A. Said R. Tarfon to him, "Aqiba, in your regard Scripture says, *He stops up streams so that they do not trickle, and what is hidden he brings into the light* (Job 28:11).

    B. "Things that are kept as mysteries from ordinary people has R. Aqiba brought to light."

"He said to him" does not make a story, and what is said does not bear the marks of a story, whole or in part.

VI: V.4

    A. Every day he would bring a bundle of twigs [Goldin: straw], half of which he would sell in exchange for food, and half of which he would use for a garment.

    B. His neighbors said to him, "Aqiba, you are killing us with the smoke. Sell them to us, buy oil with the money, and by the light of a lamp do your studying."

    C. He said to them, "I fill many needs with that bundle, first, I repeat traditions [by the light of the fire I kindle with] them, second, I warm myself with them, third, I sleep on them."

VI: V.5

    A. In time to come R. Aqiba is going to impose guilt [for failing to study] on the poor [who use their poverty as an excuse not to study].

    B. For if they say to them, "Why did you not study the Torah," and they reply, "Because we were poor," they will say to them, "But was not R. Aqiba poorer and more poverty-stricken?"

    C. If they say, "Because of our children [whom we had to work to support]," they will say to them, "Did not R. Aqiba have sons and daughters?"

    D. So they will say to them, "Because Rachel, his wife, had the merit [of making it possible for him to study, and we have no equivalent helpmates; our wives do not have equivalent merit at their disposal]."

It is hard to classify VI:V.4 as other than a narrative setting for a conversation. But the conversation makes no point by itself. In fact the whole forms a prologue to VI:V.5, which does make a powerful point.

VI:V.6

A. It was at the age of forty that he went to study the Torah. Thirteen years later he taught the Torah in public.

B. They say that he did not leave this world before there were silver and golden tables in his possession,

C. and before he went up onto his bed on golden ladders.

D. His wife went about in golden sandals and wore a golden tiara of the silhouette of the city [Jerusalem].

E. His disciples said to him, "My lord, you have shamed us by what you have done for her [since we cannot do the same for our wives]."

F. He said to them, "She bore a great deal of pain on my account for [the study of] the Torah."

This item completes the foregoing, the narrative of how Rachel's devotion to Aqiba's study of the Torah produced a rich reward. The "they said to him...he said to him..."-sequences do not comprise a story or even establish much of a narrative framework. The upshot is that for Aqiba we have a sequence of narratives but only one story, that at the beginning. The composite does not hang together very well, but it does make a few important points.

This brings us to the story of the origins, in the Torah, of Eliezer. Let us turn directly to the account:

VI:VI.1

A. How did R. Eliezer ben Hyrcanus begin [his Torah-study]?

B. He had reached the age of twenty-two years and had not yet studied the Torah. One time he said, "I shall go and study the Torah before Rabban Yohanan ben Zakkai."

C. His father Hyrcanus said to him, "You are not going to taste a bit of food until you have ploughed the entire furrow.":

D. He got up in the morning and ploughed the entire furrow.

E. They say that that day was Friday. He went and took a meal with his father in law.

F. And some say that he tasted nothing from the sixth hour on Friday until the sixth hour on Sunday.

The narrative is rather strange, since none of the actions is given a motivation. That immediately-evident difference between Eliezer's and Aqiba's story will later on prove still more striking than it does now. But it suffices to note the points in which the two stories diverge in narrative technique. While in the case of Aqiba, we know why the great master originally determined to study the Torah, in the instance of

Eliezer we do not. All we know is that at the mature age of twenty-two, he determined to study in the session of Yohanan ben Zakkai. My judgment is that the story-teller has in mind the task of explaining Eliezer's origins as Yohanan's disciple, not working out the inner motivation of the disciple. That accounts, also, for the random details, none of which fits together with the next. I see only a sequence of unintegrated details: he was twenty-two and decided to study the Torah. His father said, "Do not eat until you plough the furrow." He ploughed the furrow. Then he went and ate with his father in law. Some say he did not eat until Sunday. These details, scarcely connected, produce no effect either of narrative or of a propositional character.

VI: VI.2

    A.   On the way he saw a rock. He picked it up and too, it and put it into his mouth.
    B.   And some say that what he picked up was cattle dung.
    C.   He went and spent the night at his hostel.

Even if we read VI:VI.2 as part of VI:VI.1, all we have is more unintegrated details. Nothing in VI:VI.1-2 points to a cogent narrative, let alone a story. All we have are odd bits of information about what someone "said." The whole conglomerate does serve, however, to set the stage for VI:VI.3. The details necessary to understand what is coming have now made their appearance, and the climax is before us: he went and studied, and, because he had not eaten, produced bad breath. Yohanan recognized the bad breath and said, "Just as you suffered, so you will enjoy a reward."

VI: VI.3

    A.   He went and entered study-session before Rabban Yohanan ben Zakkai in Jerusalem.
    B.   Since a bad odor came out of his mouth, Rabban Yohanan ben Zakkai said to him, "Eliezer my son, have you taken a meal today?"
    C.   He shut up.
    D.   He asked him again, and he shut up again.
    E.,   He sent word and inquired at his hostel, and asked, "Has Eliezer eaten anything with you?"
    F.   They sent word to him, "We thought that he might be eating with my lord."
    G.   He said, "For my part, I thought that he might be eating with you. Between me and you, we should have lost R. Eliezer in the middle."
    H.   He said to him, "Just as the odor of your mouth has gone forth, so will a good name in the Torah go forth for you."

A. Hyrcanus, his father, heard that he was studying the Torah with Rabban Yohanan ben Zakkai. He decided, "I shall go and impose on Eliezer my son a vow not to derive benefit from my property."

B. They say that that day Rabban Yohanan ben Zakkai was in session and expounding [the Torah] in Jerusalem, and all the great men of Israel were in session before him. He heard that he was coming. He set up guards, saying to them, "If he es to take a seat, do not let him."

C. He came to take a seat and they did not let him.

D. He kept stepping over people and moving forward until he came to Ben Sisit Hakkesset and Naqdimon b. Gurion and Ben Kalba Sabua. He sat among them, trembling.

E. They say, On that day Rabban Yohanan ben Zakkai looked at R. Eliezer, indicating to him, "Cite an appropriate passage and give an exposition."

F. He said to him, "I cannot cite an appropriate passage."

G. He urged him, and the other disciples urged him.

H. He went and cited an opening passage and expounded matters the like of which no ear had ever heard.

I. And at every word that he said, Rabban Yohanan ben Zakkai arose and kissed him on his head and said, "My lord, Eliezer, my lord, you have taught us truth."

J. As the time came to break up, Hyrcanus his father stood up and said, "My lords, I came here only to impose a vow on my son, Eliezer, not to derive benefit from my possession. Now all of my possessions are given over to Eliezer my son, and all my other sons are disinherited and will have no share in them."

We have a beginning: Hyrcanus plans to go and place Elizer under a vow of ostracism. That not only begins the story, but it also creates an enormous tension. A dramatic setting is set up: do not let the father sit down at the back, so that the father will sit among the greatest men of Jerusalem (B-D). Yohanan then calls upon Eliezer to speak, and, after appropriate urging, he does. The tension is resolved at the climax, which also is the conclusion. I cannot think of a more perfect story, since every detail contributes to the whole, and the story-teller's intent — to underline the reward coming to the disciple, even though his family originally opposes his joining the sage — is fully realized. We note, therefore, that the conglomerate of narratives involving both Aqiba and Eliezer in fact rest in each case on a single story, and that story forms the redactional focus, permitting the aggregation of further materials, not all of them of a finished character, and some of them not stories at all.

Let us now stand back and review the whole composite involving both Aqiba and Eliezer, which, in the aggregate, makes the point that one can start Torah-study in mature years. VI:IV.1 serves only as a preface to the autonomous materials collected on the theme of how two famous masters began their studies late in life, having had no prior education. Both figures, moreover, started off poor but got rich when they became famous. These are Eliezer and Aqiba. There is no clear connection between the materials and the original saying. Perhaps the reference to wallowing in the dust of their feet in connection with Eliezer is meant to link up to the detail that he put a piece of dirt or cow dung in his mouth, but that seems to me farfetched. We refer first to Eliezer, then to Aqiba, but tell the stories in reverse order.

The diverse stories on Aqiba are hardly harmonious, since one set knows nothing of his wife, while the other introduces her as the main figure. The first set, No. 2ff., emphasizes how slow and steady wins the race. The lesson is that if one persists, one may ultimately best one's masters. No. 3 goes over the same matter, now with a parable to make the point that if one persists, he can uproot mountains. This seems to me appropriately joined to the foregoing, with the notion that Joshua and Eliezer are the mountains, as is made explicit.. Tarfon then goes over the same matter in yet another way, No. 4. No. 5 then goes over the theme of studying in poverty. No. 5 seems to me a rather pointless story, but it leads to No. 6, which presents its own message explicitly. I treat No. 6 as distinct from No. 5 because it introduces the distinct theme of Aqiba's wife, and that has nothing to do with studying in poverty, but rather, the wife's toleration of the husband's long absences. No. 7 then carries forward the second theme of the foregoing, Aqiba's wealth later on and how he lavished it on Rachel. I find puzzling the failure of the story-teller to take an interest in the source of Aqiba's great wealth. The sequence on Eliezer goes over a recurrent theme, but is as incoherent as the foregoing. No. 1 presents a number of problems of continuity, since 1.1-D are simply gibberish, there being no clear relationship between C and B. How E-F fit in I cannot say. One may make a good case for treating VI:VI.1 and VI:VI.2 as continuous. But because of the detail of 9.A, on the way he saw a rock, it seems to me that we are on good ground in treating the latter as a fragment of yet another story, rather than as a bridge. VI:VI.3 is on its own coherent and complete, a cogent and readily comprehended statement on its own. VI:VI.4 also works well, beginning to end. The details given in D then account for the appendix which follows, VI:VII-X.

V. THE PASSION OF JESUS CHRIST IN MARK'S GOSPEL AND AND THE STORY OF HOW THE SAGE DIES

Mark 14-16 tell the story of the passion, death, and resurrection of Jesus Christ. The story emphasizes the supernatural prescience of the hero, his preparation for the last supper, betrayal, sacramental deeds, distress at the prospect of suffering and death but acceptance of the father's will, trial, suffering, crucifixion, and resurrection. The narrative is not only rich, but it is full of action; the message is carried by both what is said and what is done. The range of themes and messages is remarkably broad, and, while the force of the narrative holds the whole, beginning to end, the variety of scenes and stages in the narrative yields a rich and diverse tale. It is not a tableau but a vivid sequence of events heavy with meaning. When we contrast the story of the passion of Jesus Christ as Mark (and the other evangelists) portray it with the story of the death-scenes of great sages, the representation of the Judaic saints presents a sharp contrast. If I may point to the single difference between the passion of Christ and the death of Rabbi Aqiba or Rabbi Eliezer, it is that the former is represented as an event, the latter is represented as routine and ordinary. The death of the sage serves as an occasion once again to demonstrate the serenity that study of the Torah brings to the sage: there is nothing to fear, no occasion for distress, no reason for anguish. Let us turn forthwith to the representation of sages' deaths. Here again we shall grasp why no gospels could emerge: there is nothing exceptional, nothing, really, to tell, because nothing remarkable happens, though a critical truth is once again realized. And that accounts, also, for the medium of the story, which is wholly worked out in dialogue. Where nothing happens, dialogue bears the burden of the tale.

Two moments in the life of the sage formed the center of interest: origins, meaning, beginnings as a Torah-disciple, and death. The death-stories are told under the aspect of the Torah and serve to show the supernatural power of the Torah to transform even the moment of death into an occasion of Torah-learning. The two points, start and finish, served to define and delineate the middle. How a sage coped with the death of a loved one had to draw into alignment with how a sage studied the Torah; the Torah obviously provided the model of the correct confrontation. How a sage died — the death-scene, with its quiet lessons — likewise presented a model for others. The encounter with death took narrative shape in the account of how the sage accepted comfort:

The Fathers According to Rabbi Nathan XIV:IV.1

A.   When the son of Rabban Yohanan ben Zakkai died, his disciples came in to bring him comfort.

B.   R. Eliezer came in and took a seat before him and said to him, "My lord, with your permission, may I say something before you."

C.   He said to him, "Speak."

D.   He said to him, "The first Man had a son who died, and he accepted comfort in his regard. And how do we know that he accepted comfort in his regard?

E.   "As it is said, *And Adam knew his wife again* (Gen. 4:25). You, too, be comforted."

F.   Said he to him, "Is it not enough for me that I am distressed on my own account, that you should mention to me the distress of the first Man?"

G.   R. Joshua came in and said to him, "My lord, with your permission, may I say something before you."

H.   He said to him, "Speak."

I.   He said to him, "Job had sons and daughters who died, and he accepted comfort in their regard. And how do we know that he accepted comfort in their regard?

J.   "As it is said, The Lord gave and the Lord has taken away, blessed be the name of the Lord (Job 1:21). You too, be comforted."

K.   Said he to him, "Is it not enough for me that I am distressed on my own account, that you should mention to me the distress of the Job?"

L.   R. Yose came in and took a seat before him and said to him, "My lord, with your permission, may I say something before you."

M.   He said to him, "Speak."

N.   He said to him, "Aaron had two grown-up sons who died on the same day, and he accepted comfort in their regard.

O.   "For it is said, And Aaron held his peace (Lev. 10:3),. and silence means only comfort. You too, be comforted."

P. Said he to him, "Is it not enough for me that I am distressed on my own account, that you should mention to me the distress of Aaron?"

Q. R. Simeon came in and said to him, "My lord, with your permission, may I say something before you."

R. He said to him, "Speak."

S. He said to him, "King David had a son who died, and he accepted comfort in his regard. You too, be comforted. And how do we know that he accepted comfort in his regard?

T. "As it is said, And David comforted Bath Sheba his wife and went in unto her and lay with her and she bore a son and called his name Solomon (2 Sam. 12:24).. You too, be comforted."

U. Said he to him, "Is it not enough for me that I am distressed on my own account, that you should mention to me the distress of King David?"

V. R. Eleazar b. Arakh came in. When he saw him, he said to his servant, "Take my clothes and follow me to the bathhouse [so that I can prepare to accept consolation], for he is a great man and I shall not be able to resist his arguments."

W. He came in and took a seat before him and said to him, "I shall draw a parable for you. To what may the matter be compared? To the case of a man with whom the king entrusted a treasure. Every day he would weep and cry saying, 'Woe is me, when shall I get complete and final relief from this treasure that has been entrusted to me.'

X. "You too, my lord, had a son, he recited from the Torah, Prophets and Writings, Mishnah, laws, lore, and has departed from this world without sin. You have reason, therefore, to accept consolation for yourself that you have returned your treasure, entrusted to you, whole and complete."

Y. He said to him, "R. Eleazar b. Arakh, my son, you have given comfort to me in the right way in which people console one another."

The structure of the story, focussed on the superiority of Eleazar b. Arakh (counterpart to the constructions in The Fathers 2:2ff. built along the same lines), should not obscure its larger sense. The first four disciples, Eliezer, Joshua, Yose, and Simeon, all invoke biblical models. Scripture is insufficient. Eleazar then presents an argument resting on the Oral Torah: the son had studied the Torah, inclusive of the Mishnah, laws and lore. He departed from this world without sin, so "you have returned the treasure entrusted to you." The written Torah presents a mere set of examples. The oral Torah, by contrast, provides not only the model but also the measure and the meaning. The sequence of names, to which our attention is first attracted, allows the message to be stated with great force, and the climactic statement underlines the power of the Oral Torah to define the appropriate response to the death of the child. The polemic is clear, and, we find, consistent with that of Hillel.

We come now to the stories about the death of a sage, with special reference to Yohanan ben Zakkai and his disciple, Eliezer, the only two death scenes (other than those of martyrs, below) presented in The Fathers According to Rabbi Nathan. Both death-scenes respond to lists of omens pertinent to one's condition at death. In the first, Yohanan's, there is no correspondence at all, since Yohanan is not represented as dying with a serene mind:

XXV:I.1

    A. Ben Azzai says, "Whoever has a serene mind on account of his learning has a good omen for himself, and who does not have a serene mind on account of his learning has a bad omen for himself.

    B. "Whoever has a serene mind on account of his impulse, has a good omen for himself, but [Goldin:] if his mind is distressed because of his impulse, it is a bad sign for him.

    C. "For him with whom the sages are satisfied at the hour of death it is a good sign, and for him with whom sages are not satisfied at the hour of death it is a bad sign.

    D. "For whoever has his face turned upward [at death] it is a good sign, and for whoever has his face turned toward the bed it is a bad sign.

    E. "If one is looking at people, it is a good sign, at the wall, a bad sign.

    F. "If one's face is glistening, it is a good sign, glowering, a bad one."

XXV:II.1

    A. At the time that Rabban Yohanan ben Zakkai was departing from this life, he raised up his voice and wept. His disciples said to him, "Lord, tall pillar, eternal light, mighty hammer, why are you weeping?"

    B. He said to them, "Now am I going to appear before a mortal king, who, should he be angry with me, is angry only in this world, and if he should imprison me, imposes imprisonment only in this world, and if he should put me to death, imposes death only in this world, and not only so, but whom I can appease with words and bribe with money?

    C. "Lo, I am going to appear before the King of kings of kings, the Holy One, blessed be he, who, should he be angry with me, is angry both in this world and in the world to come, whom I cannot appease with words or bribe with me.

    D. "And furthermore, before me are two paths, one to the Garden of Eden, the other to Gehenna, and I do not know on which road, whether I shall be drawn down to Gehenna or whether I shall be brought into the Garden of Eden."

    E. And in this regard it is said, *Before him shall be sentenced all those who go down to the dust, even he who cannot keep his soul alive* (Ps. 22:30).

XXV:II.2

    A. In regard to Moses Scripture says, And I will take *away my hand and you shall see my back, but my face shall not be seen* (Ex. 33:23).

    B. And further, And he *spread it before me and it was written on its face and on its back* (Ez. 2:10).

    C. *Its face* refers to this world, *its back*, to the world to come.

    D. Another interpretation: its face refers to the distress of the righteous in this world

A. *And there was written therein lamentations and jubilant sound and woe* (Ez. 2:10):

B. *Lamentations* refers to the penalty inflicted on the wicked in this world, as it is said, *This is the lamentation with which they shall lament, the daughters of the nations shall lament with it* (Ez. 32:16).

C. *...and jubilant sound and woe* refers to the reward of the righteous in the world to come, as it is said, *With an instrument of ten strings and with the psaltery, with a jubilant sound on the harp* (Ps. 92:4).

D. *...and woe:* refers to the punishment that is coming to the wicked in the world to come, as it is said, *Calamity shall come upon calamity, and rumor upon rumor* (Ez. 7:26).

XXV:II.4

A. [Yohanan ben Zakkai] would say, "Clear the house on account of uncleanness and prepare a throne for King Hezekiah of Judah."

The narrative of XXV:II.1 hardly qualifies as a story, since we have little more than a tableau: the setting of the stage, the giving of a speech. Yohanan is dying and "he said to him...he said to him...." The message is very powerful. Yohanan reminds the disciples that the judgment at hand is inexorable and incorruptible, and he does not know the way in which he will now go. The colloquy hardly qualifies as a story, and, when we come to Eliezer's, we see the possibilities for action as a vehicle for the unfolding of the narrative, characterization as a mode of making its point(s), and sustained sequences of exchange — whether word or deed — as the deep structure of the story. The essentially stationary character of the present death-scene is shown at XXV:II.2 3, which form little more than exegeses of Scripture. At XV:II.4, then, we have a further "would say" for Yohanan. These snippets scarcely qualify as a story by any definition.

XXV:III.1

A. [Ben Azzai] would say, "If one dies in a serene mind, it is a good omen from him, in derangement, it is a bad omen.

B. "...while speaking, it is a good omen, in silence, a bad omen.

C. "...in repeating words of the Torah, it is a good omen for him, in the midst of discussing business, it is a bad omen.

D. "...while doing a religious duty, it is a good omen, while involved with a trivial matter, it is a bad omen.

E. "...while happy, it is a good omen, while sad, a bad omen.

F. "...while laughing, a good omen, while weeping, a bad omen.

G. "...on the eve of the Sabbath, a good omen, at the end of the Sabbath, a bad omen.

H. "...on the eve of the Day of Atonement a bad omen, at the end of the Day of Atonement a good omen.

After the sizable interruption illustrating the first unit of the sayings, we revert to the completion of Ben Azzai's statement on this theme. A mark of the end of a systematic list is the change in the established pattern, as at H.

XXV:IV.1

A. When R. Eliezer was dying — they say it was the eve of the Sabbath [toward dusk] — R. Aqiba and his colleagues came in to see him, and he was dozing in the room, sitting back [Goldin:] on a canopied couch. They took seats in the waiting room. Hyrcanus his son came in to remove his phylacteries [which are worn on week days but not on the Sabbath, about to begin]. But he did not let him do so, and he was weeping.

B. Hyrcanus went out and said to the sages, "My lords, it appears to me that my father is deranged."

C. [Eliezer] said to him, "My son, I am not the one who is deranged, but you are the one who is deranged. For you have neglected to light the lamp for the Sabbath, on which account you may become liable to death penalty inflicted by heaven, but busied yourself with the matter of the phylacteries, on account of which liability is incurred, at worst, merely on the matter of violating the rules of Sabbath rest."

D. Since sages saw that he was in full command of his faculties, they came in and took up seats before him, but at a distance of four cubits [as was required, because Eliezer was in a state of ostracism on account of his rejection of the decision of the majority in a disputed case]. [Bringing up the case subject to dispute, so to determine whether he had finally receded to the decision of the majority,] they said to him, "My lord, as to a round cushion, a ball, [a shoe when placed on] a shoe maker's last, an amulet, and phylacteries that have been torn, what is the law as to their being susceptible to uncleanness? [Are they regarded as completed and useful objects, therefore susceptible, or as useless or incomplete and therefore not susceptible?]"

E. [Maintaining his earlier position,] he said to them, "They remain susceptible to uncleanness, and should they become unclean, immerse them as is [without undoing them, e.g., exposing their contents to the water], and take great pains in these matters, for these represent important laws that were stated to Moses at Sinai."

F. They persisted in addressed to him questions concerning matters of insusceptibility and susceptibility to uncleanness as well as concerning immersion-pools, saying to him, "My lord, what is the rule on this matter?"

G. He would say to them, "Clean."

H. And so he went, giving the answer of susceptible to uncleanness to an object that could become unclean, and insusceptible to one that could not become unclean."

I. After a while R. Eliezer said to sages, "I am amazed at the disciples of the generation, perhaps they may are liable to the death penalty at the hand of Heaven."

J. They said to him, "My lord, on what account?"

K. He said to them, "Because you never came and performed the work of apprenticeship to me."

L. Then he said to Aqiba b. Joseph, "Aqiba, on what account did you not come before me and serve as apprentice to me?"

M. He said to him, "My lord, I had no time."

N. He said to him, "I shall be surprised for you if you die a natural death."

O. And some say, He said nothing to him, but when R. Eliezer spoke as he did to his disciples, forthwith [Aqiba's] [Goldin:] heart melted within him.

P.   Said to him R. Aqiba, "My lord, how will I die?"

Q.   He said to him, "Aqiba, yours will be the worst."

XXV:IV.2

A.   R. Aqiba entered and took a seat before him and said to him, "My lord, now repeat traditions for me."

B.   He opened a subject and repeated for him three hundred rules concerning the bright spot [to which Lev. 13:1ff. refers in connection with the skin ailment translated as leprosy].

C.   Then R. Eliezer raised his two arms and and folded them on his breast and said, "Woe is me for these two arms, which are like two scrolls of Torahs, which now are departing from the world.

D.   "For were all the oceans ink, all the reeds quills, all men scribes, they could not write down what I have learned in Scripture and repeated in Mishnah-traditions, and derived as lessons from my apprenticeship to sages in the session.

E.   "Yet I have taken away from my masters only as much as does a person who dips his finger into the ocean, and I have taken away for my disciples only so much as a paintbrush takes from a paint tube.

F.   "And furthermore, I can repeat three hundred laws on the rule: *You shall not permit a sorceress to live.*"

G.   Some say, "Three thousand."

XXV:IV.3

A.   "But no one ever asked me anything about it, except for Aqiba b. Joseph.

B.   "For one time he said to me, 'My lord, teach me how people plant cucumbers and how they pull them up.'

C.   "I said something and the entire field was filled with cucumbers.'

D.   "He said to me, 'My lord, you have taught me how they are planted. Teach me how they are pulled up.'

E.   "I said something, and all of the cucumbers assembled in a single place."

XXV:IV.4

A.   Said R. Eleazar b. Azariah to him, "My lord, as to a shoe that is on the shoemaker's list, what is the law? [Is it susceptible to uncleanness, as a useful object, or insusceptible, since it is not fully manufactured and so finished as a useful object?]"

B.   He said to him, "It is insusceptible to uncleanness."

C.   And so he continued giving answers to questions, ruling of an object susceptible to uncleanness that it is susceptible, and of one insusceptible to uncleanness that it is permanently clean, until his soul went forth as he said the word, "Clean."

D.   Then R. Eleazar b. Azariah tore his clothes and wept, going forth and announcing to sages, "My lords, come and see R. Eliezer, for he is not in a state of purity as to the world to come, since his soul went forth with the word pure on his lips."

XXV:IV.5

A. After the Sabbath R. Aqiba came and found [Eliezer's corpse being conveyed for burial] on the road from Caesarea to Lud. Then he tore his clothes and ripped his hair, and his blood flowed, and he fell to the earth, crying out and weeping, saying, "Woe is me for you, my Lord, woe is me, my master, for you have left the entire generation orphaned."

B. At the row of mourners he commenced [the lament,] saying, "*My father, my father, chariot of Israel and its horsemen!* I have coins but no expert money-changer to sort them out."

The snippets of death-scenes of Eliezer are sewn together, but the distinct components are fairly easy to recognize, through the repetitions, on the one side, and the shifts in setting and premise as to the location of authorities, on the other. But the flow is smooth, beginning to end, a credit to the compiler. The detail of No. 1 becomes a main point later on, that is, the ruling on objects Eliezer had held subject to uncleanness, sages taking the opposite view. No. 1 moves along to the complaint of Eliezer that the disciples had kept their distance from him. No. 2 picks up at this point, but by introducing Aqiba, suggests that the tale is distinct from the foregoing, which already has him on the scene. The same happens later with Eleazar b. Azariah's paragraph. No. 3 then goes back over the matter of No. 2 — the distance of the disciples — and goes over its own point. No. 4 does not appear to know anything about much that has gone before, as I said, and No. 5 is independent as well, since up to now we have had Aqiba at the death scene, while here Aqiba finds out about the death only after the Sabbath and on a different set.

The story serves as a good illustration for three of the positive omens Ben Azzai has listed, while speaking, while repeating words of the Torah, and on the eve of the Sabbath. But he clearly is not represented as happy or cheerful or laughing, so, in the aggregate, I think that an illustration of the omens of Ben Azzai formed a negligible consideration in the mind of the story-tellers. The center of interest of the story is Eliezer's complaint against the disciples, who did not study Torah through service to him. The interplay of Eliezer and Aqiba then forms the centerpiece, with Nos. 1, 2, 3, and 5 placing Aqiba at the heart of matters; Eleazar b. Azariah dominates at No. 4. The materials form a nuanced and powerful story on their own. Each detail points toward the next, each sequence of action, the one to follow. The master, very much an individual and not a type, leaves a legacy of reproach, a distinctive and particular message. We have slight experience in dealing with sages as distinctive individuals, since stories over all represent them as either symbols on their own — e.g., the sage as against the emperor — or as models of virtues for the many to emulate, e.g., Hillel's patience, Yohanan b. Zakkai's resort to the Torah to cope with the destruction of the Temple.

Since the Passion-narratives deal with a martyrdom, our comparison of the

Gospel of Jesus Christ with the Torah of our sages of blessed memory requires attention to a story of the same kind. Here is how a sage's narrative is represented, once more, as an exercise in Torah-study:

XXXVIII:V.1

A. A sword comes into the world because of the delaying of justice and perversion of justice, and because of those who teach the Torah not in accord with the law.

XXXVIII:V.2

A. When they seized Rabban Simeon b. Gamaliel and R. Ishmael on the count of death, Rabban Simeon b. Gamaliel was in session and was perplexed, saying, "Woe is us! For we are put to death like those who profane the Sabbath and worship idols and practice fornication and kill."

C. Said to him R. Ishmael b. Elisha, "Would it please you if I said something before you?"

D. He said to him, "Go ahead."

E. He said to him, "Is it possible that when you were sitting at a banquet, poor folk came and stood at your door, and you did not let them come in and eat?"

F. He said to him, "By heaven [may I be cursed] if I ever did such a thing! Rather, I set up guards at the gate. When poor folk came along, they would bring them in to me and eat and drink with me and say a blessing for the sake of Heaven."

G. He said to him, "Is it possible that when you were in session and expounding [the Torah] on the Temple mount and the vast populations of Israelites were in session before you, you took pride in yourself?"

H. He said to him, "Ishmael my brother, one has to be ready to accept his failing. [That is why I am being put to death, the pride that I felt on such an occasion.]"

I. They went on appealing to the executioner for grace. This one [Ishmael] said to him, "I am a priest, son of a high priest, kill me first, so that I do not have to witness the death of my companion."

J. And the other [Simeon] said, "I am the patriarch, son of the patriarch, kill me first, so that I do not have to witness the death of my companion."

K. He said to him, "Cast lots." They cast lots, and the lot fell on Rabban Simeon b. Gamaliel.

L. The executioner took the sword and cut off his head.

M. R. Ishmael b. Elisha took it and held it in his breast and wept and cried out: "Oh holy mouth, oh faithful mouth, oh mouth that brought forth beautiful gems, precious stones and pearls! Who has laid you in the dust, who has filled your mouth with dirt and dust.

N. "Concerning you Scripture says, *Awake, O sword, against my shepherd and against the man who is near to me* (Zech. 13:7)."

O. He had not finished speaking before the executioner took the sword and cut off his head.

P. Concerning them Scripture says, *My wrath shall wax hot, and I will kill you with the sword, and your wives shall be widows, and your children fatherless* (Ex. 22:23).

The story establishes the tension at the outset: why do we die as do sinners? This question is resolved in the colloquy at C-H, at which act I concludes. The second act has the sages appeal to the executioner to spare the one the sight of the martyrdom of the other, I-L. The third and final component has Ishmael's lament: the mouth that taught the Torah will be avenged. The sage who dies in peace addresses his lessons to the Torah-community: the decline of the great tradition because of the failure of the sages and their disciples. The sage who dies as a martyr teaches a lesson of hope to Israel at large: God will ultimately exact justice of those who sin by persecuting Israel, just as God exacts strict justice even for the peccadillo of pride. The death-scenes yield a variety of lessons, since they present nuanced, and not merely conventional, portraits, with a measure of action and not merely set-piece speeches. If I had to single out the main point sages wished through the topic at hand to underline, it is God's perfect justice.

VI. INDIVIDUALITY AND CONSENSUS: FROM GOSPELS AND NAMED AUTHORS TO MISHNAH- OR SCRIPTURE-COMMENTARIES (TAL-MUDS, MIDRASH-COMPILATIONS) AND AUTHORSHIPS

Instead of authors the canonical writings of the dual Torah come from what I call authorships. Let me explain what I mean by an authorship. All classics of the Judaism of the dual Torah exhibit one definitive characteristic. It is that none is signed by a named author or is so labeled (except in a few instances long after the fact) as to represent the opinion of a lone individual. In their intrinsic traits of discourse all speak out of the single, undifferentiated voice of Sinai, and each makes a statement of the Torah of Sinai and within that Torah. That anonymity, indicative for theological reasons, comes to expression in the highly formalized rhetoric of the canonical writings, which denies the possibility of the individuation not only of the writings themselves, but also of the sayings attributed to authorities in those writings[15]. Why the sedulous anonymity of the writings of the canon of the Judaism of the dual Torah?

Books such as the Mishnah, Sifré to Deuteronomy, Genesis Rabbah, or the Bavli, that after formulation were accepted as part of the canon of Judaism, that is, of "the one whole Torah of Moses our rabbi revealed by God at Sinai," do not contain answers to questions of definition that commonly receive answers within the pages of a given book. Such authors as (the school of) Matthew or Luke, Josephus, even the writers of Ezra-Nehemiah, will have found such a policy surprising. And while Socrates did not write, Plato and Aristotle did — and they

---

[15]This is not to claim that no traits of individual speech are preserved in any canonical document. That is self-evidently false in specific instances. It is only to claim that, in general, authorships have their authorities speak in pretty much the same syntactic and grammatical patterns, with very slight provision for stylistic individuation.

[16]And, the reader should remember, where an individual opinion is given, the reason is that that opinion is thereby marked as not-normative and not to be followed. The individual is named so that the opinion may be signified as not that of the consensus. Gaining a hearing for one's ideas requires in both rhetoric and larger presentation conformity to the norms of the community and the representation of private opinon as public and anonymous.

signed their own names (or did the equivalent in context). In antiquity books or other important writings, e.g., letters and treatises, ordinarily, though not always, bore the name of the author or at least an attribution, e.g., Aristotle's or Paul's name, or the attribution to Enoch or Baruch or Luke. For no document in the canon of Judaism produced in late antiquity, by contrast, is there a named author internal to the document. No document in that canon contains within itself a statement of a clearcut date of composition, a defined place or circumstance in which a book is written, a sustained and on-going argument to which we readily gain access, or any of the other usual indicators by which we define the authorship, therefore the context and the circumstance, of a book.

Let me now give my simple reason for the phenomenon of the anonymous authorship, presenting the consensus of sages rather than the individual opinion of a single writer[16]. The purpose of the sages who in the aggregate created the canonical writings of the Judaism of the dual Torah is served by not specifying differentiating traits such as time, place, and identity of the author or the authorship. The canon — "the one whole Torah of Moses, our rabbi" — presents single books as undifferentiated episodes in a timeless, ahistorical setting: Torah revealed to Moses by God at Mount Sinai, but written down long afterward.

For reasons now spelled out, therefore, I call the framers of the document an authorship. Let me briefly expand on the importance of uncovering the fixed and public rules of orderly discourse governing any canonical book's rhetoric, logic, and topic, which, all together, permit us to describe the intent and program of those responsible for this writing: the authorship. Received in a canonical process of transmission under the auspices of a religious system, any canonical writing, by definition, enjoys authority and status within that canon and system. Hence, as I have already stressed, it is deemed to speak for a community and to represent, and contribute to, the consensus of that community. Without a named author, a canonical writing may be represented, on the surface, as the statement of a consensus. That consensus derives not from an identifiable writer or even school but from the anonymous authorities behind the document as we have it.

How do we know that a document has been so composed as to speak not for an author but for an authorship[17]? We have to ask whether this writing exhibits a cogent character and shows conformity to laws and regularities, therefore derives from a considered set of decisions of a rhetorical, logical, and topical order. If it does, then, as a matter of definition, it derives from an authorship, a collectivity that stands beyind the exhibited consensus in this particular writing. Accordingly, if I can find regularities of rhetoric, logic, and topical program, I claim to discern the consequences of rules people - an authorship - have made, decisions they have reached, concerning the character of this writing of theirs: its structure, organization,

---

[17] In answering this question, I mean to make it possible for others to replicate the results of my sustained experiments on the documents of the rabbinic canon.

[18] To be sure, we do not know — and probably never shall know — whether an authorship, as just now defined, flourished for ten days or five hundred years.

proposition, cogent statement[18]. If I find no regularities and indications of an orderly program, then I may fairly claim that this writing is different from one that speaks in behalf of people who have made rules or adopted them for the inclusion of fresh ideas of their own. It belongs in a classification not of a composition but of a scrapbook, not of a collage, which uses fixed materials in a fresh way, let alone of a sustained statement of a single system, but of a mishmash of this and that that fell together we know not how[19].

To conclude: our rapid comparison of the Gospels of Jesus Christ and the Torah of our sages of blessed memory yields a simple point of difference. Individual authors, Matthew, Mark, Luke, John, tell the story of the unique individual. A consensus of an entire community reaches its full human realization in the sage, and the writing down of that consensus will not permit individual traits of rhetoric to differentiate writer from writer or writing from writing. The individual obliterates the marks of individuality in serving the holy people by writing a work that will become part of the Torah, and stories about individuals will serve, in that context, only so far as they exemplify and realize traits characteristic of all Torah-sages. That is why, in my view, Christianity produced Gospels about a unique individual, and lives of saints later on, and that also explains why the Gospels have named authors. It also accounts for why the Judaism of the dual Torah, while valuing exemplary stories about sages, did not make provision for the counterpart, about Aqiba, of Mishnah- (and therefore also Yerushalmi- or Bavli-) tractates, or, about Eliezer, of Midrash-compilations either. While, as I have shown, the raw materials in hand, inclusive of stories about wonder-working by sages and also stories about incidents in the lives of sages, can have generated gospels or lives of saints, no one compiled the stories into biographies. It was a literary category that was excluded by the fundamental and indicative traits of the system as a whole. To state the result simply: Christianity was Christianity because of the Gospels, and Judaism was Judaism because of the Torah: different people, talking about different things, to different people. And that, by the way, also is why Talmudic Judaism had no gospels. It had what it wanted, which was, and is, the Torah of Moses, our rabbi, revealed by God at Sinai.

---

[19] I do make provision for the possibility that what looks to me like a mishmash in fact conforms to rules of cogent discourse I cannot perceive. That possibility is explored in the discussion of the rules of cogency and intelligibility, Part Two, and is further discussed in my *The Making of the Judaic Mind. The Formative Period*, in progress.

CHAPTER FIVE
GOSPEL AND MISHNAH: THE TORAH AS A SYSTEMATIC STATEMENT

My argument turns from the presence of miracle-stories and the unrealized possibility of gospels, to the presence of philosophical modes of thought and the possibility of philosophy, including natural philosophy or science, within Talmudic Judaism. The present chapter takes as its task the argument that contrasts the Gospel that the Judaism did not produce with the Mishnah that it did produce. A public document, addressed to the life of the community, the Mishnah deals not with the unique and the individual, but with the common and the communal. That is why, as a matter of fact, the Mishnah forms a highly propositional document, capable of developing syllogistic argument.

I. GOSPEL AND MISHNAH: READING THE MISHNAH AS A SYSTEMIC STATEMENT

The Mishnah contains stories, but these always serve an exemplary purpose, never addressing issues particular to the person about whom a story is told. The Mishnah's authorship's interest is not in the individual but in the community and its intent is to describe how things always are to be done, not how a given person, however holy, on his own did things. Accordingly, since, in place of Gospels of Jesus Christ, as the foundation document of Christianity, we find the Mishnah as the foundation document of Judaism, we have now to describe the counterpart, for Judaism, and its definitive and indicative traits of mind.

In defining the Mishnah, we begin with the document's topical program, because the document in excruciating detail presents a sustained exegesis of a single theme, and that is, the sanctification of Israel, the people, in its everyday life. Indeed, in the history of Judaism the Mishnah provides the single most extreme statement of the centrality of sanctification. To the authorship of the Mishnah[20], the here and now of every day life, in the natural world, forms the counterpart and opposite of the supernatural world of God in heaven, and the ordering and

---

[20]The document has no named author and contains no story of its own origins. As I shall presently point out, it starts in the middle of nowhere and ends in no determinate place. It represents a collectivity of authors, a consensus, and hence I speak of its authorship. I have demonstrated that the final formulation of all materials coincides with the penultimate processes of redaction, since a single system of forms and mnemonics is imposed on all passages uniformly. Not only so, but the document follows a carefully calibrated topical program, in which each given subject is spelled out in accord with a rigidly logical thematic program, with more important aspects of a topic treated first, less important ones later on, and, as is clear, all things treated within a single syntactic pattern. That makes unlikely the possibility that the document took shape in an incremental process, lasting over many generations, in which each generation left its deposit on the unfolding writing.

regularizing of the one in line with the main outlines of the other constitutes, for the system of the Mishnah, the labor of sanctification. That is the overriding topic, and the Mishnah's system finds cogency in the exegesis of that topic.

In its quest for the rules of order and regularity, the authorship of the Mishnah classifies and compares, finding the right rule for each matter, each important situation, by determining whether one case is like another or not like another. If it is like another, it follows the rule governing that other, and if not, it follows the opposite of that rule. In this way an orderly and logical way to sort out chaos and discover the inner order of being generates the balanced and stable, secure world described by the Mishnah. Historical events, when they enter at all, lose their one-time and unprecedented character and are shown to follow, even to generate, a fixed rule; events therefore are the opposite of eventful. This age and the age to come, history and the end of history — these categories play little role. Even the figure of the Messiah serves as a taxon, that is, a classification, namely, designation or anointment (as the word mashiah means) distinguishes one priest from another. An anointed priest — a messiah-priest — is a priest of one kind, not of some other kind. So, in all, the Mishnah's method — its process, in terms of this book — dictates the results of its authorship's thought on any given topic, including the one of salvation, which is the proposition before us. Let us now survey the Mishnah's topical program as a whole, then we turn to a brief survey of its components.

The system of philosophy expressed through concrete and detailed law presented by the Mishnah, consists of a coherent logic and topic, a cogent world view and comprehensive way of living. It is a world view which speaks of transcendent things, a way of life in response to the supernatural meaning of what is done, a heightened and deepened perception of the sanctification of Israel in deed and in deliberation. Sanctification thus means two things, first, distinguishing Israel in all its dimensions from the world in all its ways; second, establishing the stability, order, regularity, predictability, and reliability of Israel in the world of nature and supernature in particular at moments and in contexts of danger. Danger means instability, disorder, irregularity, uncertainty, and betrayal. Each topic of the system as a whole takes up a critical and indispensable moment or context of social being. Through what is said in regard to each of the Mishnah's principal topics, what the halakhic system as a whole wishes to declare is fully expressed. Yet if the parts severally and jointly give the message of the whole, the whole cannot exist without all of the parts, so well joined and carefully crafted are they all.

II. THE MISHNAH'S COGENT RHETORICAL AND LOGICAL PLAN

The dominant stylistic trait of the Mishnah, imposed in the process of ultimate closure and redaction, as I shall suggest, is the acute formalization of its syntactical structure, specifically, in its intermediate divisions, which are so organized that the limits of a theme correspond to those of a formulary pattern. The balance and order of the Mishnah are particular to the Mishnah. The Tosefta does not sustainedly reveal equivalent traits. A remarkably coherent, cogent, and exceedingly limited corpus of literary-formulaic devices and redactional conventions characterizes the document throughout. A significant single norm of agglutination predominates, which is reliance upon distinctive formulary traits imposed on a sequence of sentences and upon distinctive thematic substance expressed by these same patterned sentences. That is how intermediate units were put together and accounts also for the formalization of small ones — without reference to the diversity of authorities cited therein. Four distinctive syntactical patterns characterize all, with the fifth, the "simple declarative sentence" itself so shaped as to yield its own distinctive traits.

The relevance to the argument that the Mishnah forms a closed system is simple. If there are traces of diverse theories of formulation and redaction of materials in our division, which would reflect the individual preferences and styles of diverse circles over two hundred years, we cannot point to them. The unified and cogent formal character of the Mishnah testifies in particular to the program and plan of its ultimate tradent-redactors. We learn in the Mishnah about the intention of that last generation of Mishnaic authorities, who gave us the document as we have it. It is their way of saying things which we know for certain. The language of the Mishnah and its grammatically formalized rhetoric create a world of discourse quite separate from the concrete realities of a given time, place, or society. The exceedingly limited repertoire of grammatical patterns by which all things on all matters are said gives symbolic expression to the notion that beneath the accidents of life are a few, comprehensive relationships: unchanging and enduring patterns lie deep in the inner structure of reality and impose structure upon the accidents of the world.

III. THE MISHNAH'S COGENT TOPICAL PROGRAM

From its rhetorical and logical plan, we turn to the program of the document. Does the Mishnah in its contents emerge from a continuous and linear and incremental process of oral tradition, so that we may turn to the Mishnah for lessons on that process? I have thus far emphasized matters of form, form-analysis, rhetoric, and cogency of discourse. But what about the contents of the document? Do these come to the framers of the Mishnah in a process of oral tradition? Are these the product of historical tradition at all? To state the question still more broadly, is the Mishnah the statement of a tradition or does it present the statement of a system, made up all at once? If the answer proves to be that we have the statement of a system, then we see what it means to treat a document on its own terms. And, at that point, the question emerges concerning how we are to identify that larger system of which after the fact the documentary system forms a component.

I may frame matters in a simple way. Does the Mishnah derive from an agglutinative process of traditional formulation and transmission of an intellectual heritage, facts and thought alike? Or does that document make a statement of its own, cogent and defined within the requirements of an inner logic, proportion, and structure, imposing that essentially autonomous vision upon whatever materials its authorship has received from the past? On the one side, as I shall now make clear, the Mishnah does make use of received materials. But on the other, we have seen that in literary terms the Mishnah is not traditional, formed out of the increment of received materials, the form of the reception of which governs, but — in the sense now implied — systemic, that is, again in literary terms orderly, systematic, laid out in a proportion and order dictated by the inner logic of a topic or generative problem and — and therefore — authoritative by reason of its own rigorous judgment of issues of rationality and compelling logic, then I can offer a reasonable hypothesis resting on facts of literature.

IV. THE LAWS OF THE MISHNAH AND THE MISHNAH'S STATEMENT: LINEAR HISTORY OR SYSTEMATIC STATEMENT?

To explain the history of the Mishnah's laws, we have to recall a simple fact. Apart from the scriptural law codes, in antiquity no single system of law governed all Jews everywhere. So we cannot describe "Jewish law" as one encompassing system, everywhere handed down as tradition from generation to generation. The Scripture's several codes of course made their impact on the diverse systems of law that governed various groups of Jews, or Jewish communities in various places. But that impact never proved uniform. In consequence, in no way may we speak of "Jewish law," meaning a single legal code or even a common set of encompassing rules everywhere held authoritative by Jewry. The relationship between the legal system of one distinct group of Jews to that governing some other proves various.

Certain practices to be sure characterized all. But these too do not validate the premise that such a thing as "Jewish law" operated, even in the points in common, pretty much everywhere. The fact that Jews ordinarily observed certain taboos, e.g., concerning the Sabbath day and forbidden foods, hardly changes the picture. On the basis of the prohibition of pork and the observance of a common calendar one can hardly describe a common law of Jewry, hence "Jewish law." Such evidence as we have of diverse Jews' laws points in the opposite direction. What these sets of laws shared in common in part derives from the Scripture all revered. What turns up in a number of contexts in further measure proves so general or so fragmentary as to yield no trace of a single, systematic and comprehensive law common among Jews. An example of the latter — something too general to make much difference — is the marriage-contract. It is a fact that marriage-contracts occur in the Jewish community records of Elephantine, in the fragments found from the time of Bar Kokhba, and in the setting of Mishnaic law. But in detail the contracts that have been found scarcely intersect. The Mishnah's rules governing the scribal preparation of such contracts hardly dictated to the authorities of fifth century B.C. Elephantine or second century C.E. Palestine how to do their work. When, therefore, we wish to investigate the history of Jewish law, in point of fact we must follow the course of distinct bodies of sources. Each of these several systems of law applying to diverse

Jewish groups or communities emerges from its distinct historical setting, addresses its own social entity, and tells us, usually only in bits and pieces of detailed information, about itself alone.

The fact is that much of the law of the Mishnah derives from the age before its final closure. In that sense, the Mishnah presents us with the results of a process of tradition. In the Mishnah we see how a group of jurisprudents drew together a rich heritage of legal and moral traditions and facts and made of them a single system. From Scripture onward, no other composition compares in size, comprehensive treatment of a vast variety of topics, balance, proportion, and cogency. Let us rapidly review the various types of evidence for the antiquity of numerous facts utilized by the Mishnah's framers in the construction of their system.

Some legal facts in the Mishnah, as in other law codes of its place and age, derive from remote antiquity. Categories of law and investment, for instance, prove continuous with Akkadian and even Sumerian ones. It has been shown that the linguistic and legal datum of Mishnah's rules goes back to Assyrian law. Other important continuities in the common law of the ancient Near East have emerged in a broad diversity of research, on Elephantine law for instance. The issue therefore cannot focus upon whether or not the Mishnah in diverse details draws upon established rules of jurisprudence. It assuredly does. Yet another mode of demonstrating that facts in the Mishnah's system derive from a period substantially prior to that in which the Mishnah reached closure carries us to the data provided by documents redacted long before the Mishnah. For one example, details of rules in the law codes found in the library of the Essene community of Qumran intersect with details of rules in the Mishnah. More interesting still, accounts of aspects of Israelite life take for granted that issues lively in the Mishnah came under debate long before the closure of the Mishnah. The Gospels' accounts of Jesus' encounter with the Pharisees, among others, encompass rules of law, or topics dealt with, important to the Mishnah. It is, for instance, not merely the datum that a writ of divorce severs the tie between wife and husband. The matter of grounds for divorce proves important to sages whose names occur in the Mishnah, and one position of one of these sages turns out to accord with the position on the same matter imputed to Jesus. It follows that not only isolated facts but critical matters of jurisprudential philosophy came to the surface long before the closure of the Mishnah.

That fact yields one incontrovertible result. The Mishnah's rules have to come into juxtaposition, wherever possible, with the rules that occur in prior law codes, whether Israelite or otherwise. That is the case, even though it presently appears that only a small proportion of all of the rules in the Mishnah fall within the frame of prior documents, remote or proximate. For every rule we can parallel in an earlier composition, the Mishnah gives us dozens of rules that in topic, logic or even mere detail bear no comparison to anything now known in a prior composition, from Sumerian and Akkadian to Essene and Christian writers alike. (The sole exception, the Hebrew Scripture's law codes, comes under analysis in the next section.) Details of the law, wherever possible, still must stand in comparison with equivalent details in earlier documents, whether narrative or legislative. In that way we gain perspective on what, in the Mishnah, has come into the framers hands from an earlier period. At stake in such perspective is insight into the mind of the Mishnah's framers and the character of their system. We see what they have made out of available materials. What do we learn from the occurrence of facts by the time of the Mishnah more than two millenia old, or of issues important two centuries earlier? We review the resources selected by those who contributed to the traditions brought to closure in the Mishnah. We know as fact that the Mishnah's authorship drew on received information. But did they formulate their document as a restatement of that information, that tradition? That is a separate question.

For the authors of the Mishnah in using available, sometimes very ancient, materials, reshaped whatever came into their hands. The document upon close reading proves systematic and orderly, purposive and well composed. It is no mere scrapbook of legal facts, arranged for purposes of reference. It is a document in which — just as in the traits of rhetorical and formal composition — the critical problematic at the center always exercises influence over the peripheral facts, dictating how they are chosen, arranged, utilized. So even though some facts in the document prove very old indeed, on that basis we understand no more than we did before we knew that some facts come from ancient times. True law as the Mishnah presents law derives from diverse sources, from remote antiquity onward. But the law as it emerges whole and complete in the Mishnah, in particular, that is, the system, the structure, the proportions and composition, the topical program and the logical and syllogistic whole — these derive from the imagination and wit of the final two generations, in the second century C.E., of the authors of the Mishnah.

A simple exercise will show that, whatever the antiquity of rules viewed discretely, the meaning and proportionate importance of rules taken all together derive from the perspective and encompassing theory of the authors of the Mishnah themselves. That is what will show that the history of law as the Mishnah presents the law, can be traced, whole and cogent, only within the data of the Mishnah itself: systemically, not episodically. The desired exercise brings us to the relationship of the Mishnah to Scripture. For, as noted just now, that is the one substantial source to which the authors of the Mishnah did make reference. Accordingly, to demonstrate the antiquity of more than discrete and minor details of law of the Mishnah, we turn to Scripture. There, it is clear, we can find out whether the Mishnah constitutes merely a repository of ancient law.

Indeed, proof of the claim that there was not merely law characteristic of a given group, but the law, shared by "all Israel," should derive solely from the Scripture common to all Israel everywhere. How so? The theory of a single, continuous law rests upon the simple fact that all Israel by definition acknowledged the authority of Scripture, its law and theology. It must follow that, in diverse ways and within discrete exegetical processes, every group now known to us drew its basic legal propositions from Scripture and therefore contributes evidence on the unilinear formation of a single law, based upon a single source, common to all Israel, that is, the law or law. In examining the notion of the law, as distinct from the theory, argued here, of diverse systems of law, we turn to the critical issue. It concerns not whether a given rule derives from exegesis of Scripture. That issue, by itself, provides trivial and not probative insight. Rather we want to know how the several systems now known to us define their respective relationships to Scripture. That is to say, we ask about the nature of Scriptural authority, the use of Scripture's facts in a code, or system, of law. The answer to the question settles an important issue. If two (or more) systems of law governing groups of Israelites turn out to respond to, to draw upon, Scripture's rules in much the same way, then these discrete systems merge at their roots, in a generative and definitive aspect of their structure. In consequence, we may conclude the two (or more) systems do form part of a single common law, once more, the law. But if two or more systems of law approach Scripture each in its own way and for its own purposes, then we have to analyze each system on its own terms and not as part of, and contributory to, the law.

V. SYSTEM AND SELECTIVITY: THE USES OF SCRIPTURE

For the present purpose it will suffice to demonstrate one modest fact. The authors of the Mishnah read Scripture, as they read much else, in terms of the system and structure they proposed to construct. Their goals and conceptions told them what, in Scripture, they would borrow, what they would expand and articulate, what they would acknowledge but neglect and what they would simply ignore. That fact shows that law in the Mishnah, even though shared here and there with other codes, and even though intersecting with still other systems, constitutes a distinct and autonomous system of law, a law on its own. So, to review, the Mishnah then does not absorb and merely portray in its own way established rules of law out of a single, continuous and cogent legal system, the law. Why not? Because, as we shall now see, the Mishnah's authors turn out to have taken from Scripture what they chose in accord with the criterion of the one thing they wished to accomplish. This was the construction of their system of law with its distinctive traits of topical and logical composition: *their* law, not *the* law.

In order to show the preeminence, in the encounter with Scripture's laws, of the perspective and purpose of the authors of the Mishnah, we simply review the Mishnah's tractates and ask how, overall, we may characterize their relationships to Scripture. Were these wholly dependent, wholly autonomous, or somewhere in-between? That is, at the foundations in fact and generative problematic of a given tractate, we may discover nothing more than facts and interests of Scripture's law. The tractate's authors may articulate the data of Scripture. Or when we reach the bed rock of a tractate, the point at which the articulation of the structure of the tractate rests, we may find no point of contact with facts, let alone interests, of Scriptures laws. And, third, we may discover facts shared by Scripture but developed in ways distinctive to the purposes of the framers of the Mishnah-tractate at hand. These three relationships, in theory, encompass all possibilities. Let us turn to the facts.

First, there are tractates which simply repeat in their own words precisely what Scripture has to say, and at best serve to amplify and complete the basic ideas of Scripture. For example, all of the cultic tractates of the Second Division, the one on Appointed Times, which tell what one is supposed to do in the Temple on the various special days of the year, and the bulk of the cultic tractates of the Fifth Division, which deals with Holy Things, simply restate facts of Scripture. For another example all of those tractates of the Sixth Division, on Purities, which specify sources of uncleanness, depend completely on information supplied by Scripture. Every important statement in Niddah, on menstrual uncleanness, and the most fundamental notions of Zabim, on the uncleanness of the person with flux referred to in Lev. 15, as well as every detail in Negaim, on the uncleanness of the person or house suffering the uncleanness described at Lev. 13 and 14 — all of these tractates serve only to restate the basic facts of Scripture and to complement those facts with other important ones.

There are, second, tractates which take up facts of Scripture but work them out in a way in which those Scriptural facts cannot have led us to predict. A supposition concerning what is important about the facts, utterly remote from the supposition of Scripture, will explain why the Mishnah tractates under discussion say the original things they say in confronting those Scripturally provided facts. For one example, Scripture takes for granted that the red cow will be burned in a state of uncleanness, because it is burned outside the camp, meaning the Temple. The priestly writers cannot have imagined that a state of cultic cleanness was to be attained outside of the cult. The absolute datum of tractate Parah, by contrast, is that cultic cleanness not only can be attained outside of the "tent of meeting." The red cow was to be burned in a state of cleanness exceeding even that cultic cleanness required in the Temple itself. The problematic which generates the intellectual agendum of Parah, therefore, is how to work out the conduct of the rite of burning the cow in relationship to the Temple: Is it to be done in exactly the same way, or in exactly the opposite way? This mode of contrastive and analogical thinking helps us to understand the generative problematic of such tractates as Erubin and Besah, to mention only two.

And third, there are, predictably, many tractates which either take up problems in no way suggested by Scripture, or begin from facts at best merely relevant to facts of Scripture. In the former category are Tohorot, on the cleanness of foods, with its companion, Uqsin; Demai, on doubtfully tithed produce; Tamid, on the conduct of the daily whole offering; Baba Batra, on rules of real estate transactions and certain other commercial and property relationships, and so on. In the latter category are Ohalot, which spins out its strange problems with the theory that a tent and a utensil are to be compared to one another (!); Kelim, on the susceptibility to uncleanness of various sorts of utensils; Miqvaot, on the sorts of water which effect purification from uncleanness, and many others. These tractates draw on facts of Scripture. But the problems confronted in these tractates in no way respond to problems important to Scripture. What we have here is a prior program of inquiry, which will make ample provision for facts of Scripture in an inquiry to begin with generated essentially outside of the framework of Scripture.

Some tractates merely repeat what we find in Scripture. Some are totally independent of Scripture. Some fall in between. Scripture confronts the framers of the Mishnah as revelation, not merely as a source of facts. But the framers of the Mishnah had their own world with which to deal. They made statements in the framework and fellowship of their own age and generation. They were bound, therefore, to come to Scripture with a set of questions generated elsewhere than in Scripture. They brought their own ideas about what was going to be important in Scripture. This is perfectly natural.

The philosophers of the Mishnah conceded to Scripture the highest authority. At the same time what they chose to hear, within the authoritative statements of Scripture, will in the end form a statement of its own. To state matters simply: all of Scripture is authoritative. But only some of Scripture is relevant. And what happened is that the framers and philosophers of the tradition of the Mishnah came to Scripture when they had reason to. That is to say, they brought to Scripture a program of questions and inquiries framed essentially among themselves. So they were highly selective. Their program itself constituted a statement upon the meaning of Scripture. They and their apologists of one sort hastened to add, their program consisted of a statement of and not only upon the meaning of Scripture.

The authority of Scripture therefore for the Mishnah is simply stated. Scripture provides indisputable facts. It is wholly authoritative — *once we have made our choice of which part of Scripture we shall read.* Scripture generated important and authoritative structures of the community, including disciplinary and doctrinal statements, decisions, and interpretations — once people had determined which part of Scripture to ask to provide those statements and decisions. Community structures envisaged by the Mishnah were wholly based on Scripture — when Scripture had anything to lay down. But Scripture is not wholly and exhaustively expressed in those structures which the Mishnah does borrow. Scripture has dictated the character of formative structures of the Mishnah. But the Mishnah's system is not the result of the dictation of close exegesis of Scripture, except after the fact.

The traits of rhetoric and logical cogency we have examined yield one result. The Mishnah's formulation derives from the work of redaction. So we cannot show that sizable components of the Mishnah were written down, pretty much as we have them, long before the closure of the document as a whole. On formal and literary grounds, the opposite is the fact: most of the Mishnah conforms to a single program of formulation, and that set of rules on formulation derives from encompassing

81

decisions concerning redaction. But what about the history of the law and its formation into the system we now have? As a matter of fact, details of the system of the Mishnah's law emerge, within the final document at attributions that withstand a simple test of verification to figures who flourished at the turn of the first century A.D., though details, commonly routine facts of a common law, may originate as much as two thousand years earlier than that. From that point onward, there is in the Mishnah a process of tradition? The law of the Mishnah takes shape in a twofold process. Once a theme is introduced early in the history of law, it will be taken up and refined later on. Also, in the second and third stages in the formation of the Mishnah, after the destruction of the Templ in A.D. 70 and then after the defeat of Bar Kokhba in A.D. 135, many new themes with their problems will emerge. These however are without precedent in the antecedent thematic heritage. The common foundations for the whole always are Scripture, of course, so that I may present a simple architectural simile.

The law of the Mishnah is like a completed construction of scaffolding. The foundation is a single plane, the Scriptures. The top platform also is a single plane, the Mishnah itself. But the infrastructure is differentiated. Underneath one part of the upper platform will be several lower platforms, so that the supporting poles and pillars reach down to intervening platforms; only the bottom platform rests upon pillars set in the foundation. Yet another part of the upper platform rests upon pillars and poles stretching straight down to the foundation, without intervening platforms at all. So viewed from above, the uppermost platform of the scaffolding forms a single, uniform, and even plane. That is the Mishnah as we have it, six Divisions, sixty-three tractates, five hundred thirty-one chapters. But viewed from the side, that is, from the perspective of analysis, there is much differentiation, so that, from one side, the upper platform rises from a second, intermediate one, and, in places, from even a third, lowest one. And yet some of the pillars reach directly down to the bedrock foundations.

What is new in the period beyond the wars is that part of the ultimate plane — the Mishnah as a whole — which in fact rests upon the foundations not of antecedent thought but of Scripture alone. What is basic in the period before 70 A.D. is the formation of that part of the Mishnah which sustains yet a second and even a third layer of platform construction. What emerges between the two wars, of course, will both form a plane with what comes before, that platform at the second level, and yet will also lay foundations for a level above itself. But this intermediate platform also will come to an end, yielding that space filled only by the pillars stretching from Scripture on upward to the ultimate plane of the Mishnah's completed and whole system.

VI. THE MISHNAH AS PHILOSOPHICAL SYSTEM, NOT INCREMENTAL TRADITION

The legal system presented by the Mishnah consists of a coherent logic and topic, a cogent world view and comprehensive way of living. It is a world view which speaks of transcendent things, a way of life in response to the supernatural meaning of what is done, a heightened and deepened perception of the sanctification of Israel in deed and in deliberation. Each topic of the system as a whole takes up a critical and indispensable moment or context of social being. Through what is said in regard to each of the Mishnah's principal topics, what the legal system as a whole wishes to declare is fully expressed. Yet if the parts severally and jointly give the message of the whole, the whole cannot exist without all of the parts, so well joined and carefully crafted are they all. And that yields the main point of this brief summary of fifteen years of research. Gospels tell stories and invoke history. The Mishnah does not. And there is a good reason for the difference. I state the result with emphasis:

Viewed as a whole, the Mishnah's system has no history and does not derive from an incremental process of tradition. But seen piece by piece, the principal components of the system do emerge from such a traditional process. The difference, as I believe I have shown in the monograph at hand, is that the Mishnah, whole and complete, emerged from a process of formulation and transmission accomplished by a cogent social group, who knew precisely the rules of rhetoric and logic they wished to impose on the presentation of any topic at hand.

The Mishnah therefore is a systemic and states a philosophical system, whole and complete, — that and not a traditional document. It emerged as a whole and complete statement, deriving information from earlier generations, information preserved in a variety of ways. That is all we can say as a matter of literary-historical fact. The Mishnah is a systemic, and not a traditional, statement and document. In the model of the Mishnah I should furthermore claim that the canonical documents of formative Judaism may constitute, each on its own, statements at the end of a sustained process of rigorous thought and logical inquiry, applied logic and practical reason. The only way to read a reasoned and systematic statement of a system is defined by the rules of general intelligibility, the laws of reasoned and syllogistic discourse about rules and principles. The way to read a traditional and sedimentary document by contrast lies through the ad hoc and episodic display of instances and examples, layers of meaning and eccentricities of confluence, intersection, and congruence. That is why, for my part I maintain that tradition and system cannot share a single crown, and that, the formative documents of Judaism demonstrate, Judaism constitutes not a traditional but a systemic religious statement, with a hermeneutics of order, proportion, above all, reasoned context, to tell us how to read each document. We cannot read these writings in accord with two incompatible hermeneutical programs, and, for reasons amply stated, I argue in favor of the philosophical and systemic, rather than the agglutinative and traditional, hermeneutics.

Whatever happens to thought, whatever the sources of received information ("tradition"), in the mind of the thinker ideas come to birth cogent, whole, complete

—and on their own. Extrinsic considerations of context and circumstance play their role, but logic, cogent discourse, rhetoric, — these enjoy an existence, an integrity too. If sentences bear meaning on their own, then to insist that sentences bear meaning only in line with friends, companions, partners in meaning contradicts the inner logic of syntax that, on its own, imparts sense to sentences. These are the choices: everything imputed, as against an inner integrity of logic and the syntax of syllogistic thought[22]. As between the philosophical heritage of Athens and any other hermeneutics, I maintain that the authorities of the Mishnah demonstrate the power of the philosophical reading of the one whole Torah of Moses, our rabbi. And, further, I should propose that the reason for sages' remarkable success in persuading successive generations of Israel of the Torah's ineluctable truth lies not in arguments from tradition, from "Sinai," so much as in appeals to the self-evidence of the well-framed argument, the well-crafted sentence of thought.

The literature of Judaism, exemplified by the Mishnah, commonly finds representation as wholly continuous, so that everything always testifies to the meaning of everything else, and, moreover, no book demands or sustains a reading on its own. It is represented as traditional, as an example of oral tradition. So it is — as to its future, not as to its origins. The authorship at hand worked at the outset, de novo. They were philosophers in the deepest and richest sense of the tradition of philosophy. The Mishnah's authorship presents a profoundly reasoned view of a rational and well-proportioned world, a world of rules and order and reason and rationality. That constitutes their religious statement: the affirmation of creation as a work of logic and order and law, to which the human mind, with its sense of logic, order, and rule, conforms, as it was created to conform. And that is why Talmudic Judaism did not make gospels: because it did not have to, since it already had the Torah.

---

[22]No one can maintain that the meanings of words and phrases, the uses of syntax, bear meanings wholly integral to discrete occasions. Syntax works because it joins mind to mind, and no mind invents language. But that begs the question and may be dismissed as impertinent, since the contrary view claims far more than the social foundation of the language.

INDEX